W9-CHK-029

101
questions

What's bothering your dog and how to solve its problems

your dog would ask

Helen Dennis
VetMB MRCVS

BARNES & NOBLE
NEW YORK

Contents

1 Getting a New Dog 8

2 Daily Care 28

Introduction

Over the past few decades, the role of dogs as pets has changed. Most dogs now have a firm place within the home, living in the house and sharing in family life. They are

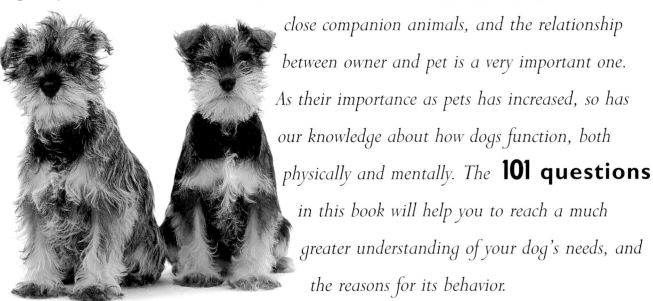

close companion animals, and the relationship between owner and pet is a very important one. As their importance as pets has increased, so has our knowledge about how dogs function, both physically and mentally. The **101 questions** in this book will help you to reach a much greater understanding of your dog's needs, and the reasons for its behavior.

We want our dogs to be happy, healthy, and well-behaved. A dog that is all these things is the perfect companion and a pleasure to live with. However, achieving this ideal pet is not as easy as it might seem.

The **101 questions** in this book cover many aspects of canine behavior, communication, and care. They will help you to train your dog effectively but with kindness, and to keep your dog healthy and happy, so that you and your dog can share a mutually satisfying relationship for many years to come.

Why did you choose me as your new dog

Why are you taking me to the veterinarian

What are you going to feed me

Why can't I sleep on your bed at night

I get bored on my own. May I have some toys

SPECIAL FEATURE: Playtime

What if there's a cat in my new home

What's a puppy party

Why can't I go to the bathroom indoors

Getting a New Dog

The arrival of a new dog is an exciting time for both pet and owner, and there is a lot for the new dog to learn. Training with kindness, praise, and an understanding of canine behavior can produce a well-adjusted dog that is happy and content, and a pleasure to live with.

Why did you choose me as your new dog?

A Acquiring a dog is a big decision, and involves making a number of choices. One of the first is whether to get a puppy or an older dog. Puppies are wonderful fun, but they are also hard work. A newly acquired puppy needs someone with it much of the day, so that it can get to know its new family. The early months are also a very important training time. Someone needs to be there to educate and encourage the puppy to develop good behavior patterns, and it is vital that someone is around to take the puppy outside frequently before it is housebroken.

An older dog will already be housebroken, and may be quite happy left on its own for some of the time. However, it may have behavioral problems that are difficult to modify. These may be the result of a traumatic past, since many abused dogs have behavioral as well as physical problems. One big advantage of taking on a mature dog, however, is that you do know the dog's final size!

The Right Choice

To maximize the chances of a long and happy life with your new dog, try to choose a breed and temperament that fits your lifestyle.

Purebred or mixed breed? A purebred dog has parents of the same breed and will grow to resemble them in size and characteristics. It can be difficult to predict the eventual size or the temperament of a mixed breed puppy. Always ask to see the mother – the father is unlikely to be around! Find out as much as you can about your potential pet's parents. Are they noisy, yappy, inclined to run off? Can they be trusted with children? Other dogs?

Male or female? Dogs and bitches can differ in size and character. The males of small breeds such as some terriers can be highly sexed, and the males of larger breeds tend to be bigger and more combative than the females. Bitches are generally easier to train, but can become moody when they are in heat and can suffer from false pregnancies. Male dogs may wander in search of females.

? What information did you get on my breed?

All breeds of dog have good traits and bad traits. Like humans, none is perfect. A veterinarian or a breeder can supply information about the traits of any particular breed. They will also be able to advise about possible hereditary disease problems, which are an important consideration with purebred dogs. If acquiring a purebred, be sure to see the health papers of the parents, for example, the results of eye tests and hip X-rays.

Why are you taking me to the veterinarian?

A A health examination is advisable for any new dog. In addition to making sure that the dog is generally fit, the veterinarian can check for hereditary diseases. The veterinarian will know the diseases to which a particular breed is prone, examine the dog for early signs, and give advice about possible future symptoms. This first visit is a good opportunity to discuss diet, worming, insurance, and any other health issues.

? Will the veterinarian give me an injection?

Puppies gain immunity to many diseases from antibodies in their mother's milk. However, this immunity gradually wanes. Puppies can then gain immunity either by direct exposure to a disease, which can be dangerous, or by vaccination. If a puppy is well at its first checkup (usually at about eight weeks of age), a vaccination course can be started. The injection is given into the scruff of the neck, and is not painful. However, the dog may be a little quiet for the next day or so. Protection against disease by early vaccination means a puppy can mix with other dogs and humans — an important part of its development — from about a week after its first injection.

Happy Travels

If puppies are introduced to car trips with reassurance, travel soon becomes less worrying. You can also teach your dog to associate car rides with something pleasant, such as a trip to the park, so that your dog will look forward to traveling.

Dogs often feel happier in the car if held securely by someone, or made comfortable in a travel cage. Limit drives to a few minutes at first, and return home to a meal. Gradually increase the length of the journeys, taking your dog to a place that it enjoys.

If your dog is reluctant to get into the car, tempt it with a tasty tidbit, and when it does get in, give the dog lots of praise.

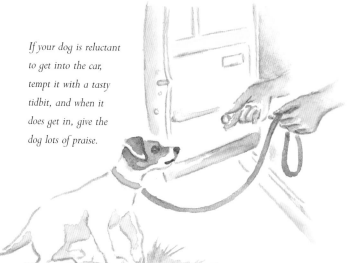

Always make sure the car is well-ventilated. If this means opening a window, do not open it so wide that the dog is able to put its head outside, as this can be dangerous. Never leave your dog alone in a parked car — even in cool weather, a car can become an oven in a matter of minutes, and the dog can overheat and die.

? Will I throw up in the car?

Many puppies are car sick. They salivate profusely, and sooner or later vomit. The majority outgrow this problem by the time they are a year old. There are two main reasons for a dog being a poor traveler: fear and excitement. The sound of the engine and the movement of the car can be a very frightening experience for a young puppy. Medication for motion sickness can be prescribed by a veterinarian.

what are you going to feed me.

Puppies have special dietary requirements. They need energy for maintenance and activity, and also materials for growth. In fact, a young puppy needs two to three times as much food as an adult dog of the same weight. The best food to give a puppy is one of the many brands that are especially formulated to meet a puppy's nutritional needs. These foods contain a higher percentage of calories, protein, and minerals, such as calcium and phosphorus, than adult dog foods. The correct amount to feed varies with different foods, but the packaging will carry recommendations. Overfeeding will lead to diarrhea.

? When will I get my grown-up teeth?

Puppies' milk teeth start to emerge at about two weeks of age. By eight weeks, they should have all their temporary puppy teeth – 28 in total. There are no molar teeth in this set. Temporary teeth are replaced by permanent teeth at four to six months. A dog has 42 permanent teeth. At the time of "teething," puppies may develop sore gums and go through a stage of chewing. Occasionally, despite the emergence of permanent teeth, some temporary teeth remain in place. These sometimes need to be removed by a veterinarian, particularly in small breeds, as they can cause the new teeth to grow in an abnormal direction.

? Can you catch anything from me?

Most young puppies have parasites of some sort, such as fleas and worms. They should be treated for these, because they are detrimental to the health of the puppy and can affect humans, although normal hygienic practices will usually eliminate this possibility. One major health concern is a worm known as *toxocara canis*. Accidental ingestion of toxocara eggs, although rare, can result in human infection. Occasional cases of blindness have occurred. The stress of moving to a new home or a sudden change in diet can cause diarrhea in young dogs. When the diarrhea is caused by bacteria, humans can become infected. Good hygiene will prevent human illness. Sensible precautions include wearing gloves when cleaning up mess, and always washing hands after stroking and handling the dog. Dogs should not be allowed to lick children's faces.

Puppy Diet

Although puppies need large amounts of food in relation to their size, they only have small-capacity stomachs.

At two months of age puppies need four to five small meals a day. By three months, they can be fed three times a day, and this can be reduced to one or two meals by the time they are a year old.

Puppies can have dried or canned food, or a combination of both. Dried foods can be soaked at first, until the puppy is able to enjoy crunching them. They should be small enough for the puppy to do this.

If a puppy is fed a complete puppy diet, there is no need to give mineral and vitamin supplements. Milk is not essential, but can be given in small quantities.

Why can't I sleep on your bed

A There are two major reasons for not allowing a dog to sleep on its owner's bed: health and behavior. Dogs can be afflicted by skin parasites, such as fleas and ticks, which are just as happy to bite humans as, dogs. They can also have worms, the segments of which can be deposited on the bedding. Many owners are prepared to accept this risk, especially if the dog is regularly wormed, for the pleasure of having close contact with their pet.

Behavioral problems related to sharing the owner's bed are those of dominance and overdependence. For owner and dog to coexist happily, the owner needs to be dominant. This is more important with some dogs than others. In the case of strong-willed dogs that need constant reminding of their place in the "pack," namely below all human family members, dominance can be asserted by not allowing the dog into the owner's den – that is, his or her bedroom. If possible, the dog should not be allowed upstairs at all.

The constant presence of an owner can cause a dog to become overdependent, and very unhappy when left alone. It is important that a dog be trained from puppyhood to accept times alone, otherwise it will develop separation-anxiety problems.

? What's this metal cage for?

A house cage or indoor kennel is a collapsible metal cage that can easily be moved from room to room. The dog's bed can be put in it, and it can become the dog's den, a place of safety and protection. A cage helps in housebreaking – a dog never willingly soils its bed – and prevents chewing and other destructive habits. The dog can be left in the cage when the owner goes out, or when, for some reason, the dog needs to be confined. Appropriate toys can be placed in the kennel.

Bedtime

Every dog is different, and owners should follow their inclinations when deciding where a dog sleeps.

at night

Every dog needs its own bed, which will be a place where the dog feels safe and secure, and which can be its den. A practical bed is made of hard plastic, is fairly resistant to chewing, and can be washed. Nice, soft bedding can be put into it.

Some puppies and dogs initially need close contact with their new owners. Their bed can be placed next to yours. As the dog becomes more settled, the bed can gradually be moved out of the room, and the dog can learn to sleep wherever is most convenient.

? . I get bored on my own. May I have

A

It is natural for puppies to play and to chew, and this behavior continues in many dogs into old age. If puppies are not provided with toys, they will make their own, and these can be furniture, wallpaper, children's toys, sticks, and stones. Use of such items can be hazardous to the dog and distressing to the owner, so providing safe and enjoyable toys for the dog is the perfect solution.

? Why can't I bite you when we're playing together?

Young puppies in a litter play physical games with their brothers, sisters, and parents, often using teeth to tug at ears and tails. As their teeth grow larger and sharper, this becomes unacceptable to the other dogs, who teach the puppy by their reactions to modify the use of teeth in play. This process is complete by four to five months of age. When puppies leave their littermates, their new, human family have to continue this education. It is an extremely important part of the puppy's training. Playbiting can progress to very boisterous play, which can be dangerous, especially where large dogs are concerned.

some toys !

? What *kind of toys are you going to buy me?*

There are many excellent dog toys available, including objects for chewing, toys to help clean teeth, and playthings that require the owner's participation, such as tuggers and rubber rings. Chewing toys will help to occupy a dog that is on its own, and can be offered whenever the dog shows interest in household items, such as carpets and shoes.

No Biting

A dog that bites people can soon learn to use this power to control its family. It becomes a danger, especially to children. Many dogs each year are euthanized for biting.

To stop this behavior, whenever the dog uses its teeth during play, say "No!" in a firm tone of voice. Then walk off and ignore the dog for five minutes. If the dog persists, put it in its cage or send it to another room for a short while. Biting is often an attention-seeking device, and the dog will soon learn that nipping is counterproductive.

All members of the family must adopt the same attitude in training. It is no good scolding the dog for biting children if an adult then engages in a rough game with the dog and allows it to use its teeth.

SPECIAL

FEATURE

Playtime

Playfulness is part of the great appeal of dogs as pets. Playing together helps to form the relationship between the dog and its human family.

Play is also an important part of a dog's development, because it stimulates a dog both physically and mentally, and helps to shape its behavior and communication skills. Playing with a dog should therefore start when it is a puppy. Those dogs that haven't had this experience as puppies are often very serious older dogs that never learn to play.

Different Games

Different breeds of dog enjoy different types of games. For example, terriers like predatory games that simulate the catching and killing of prey; collies enjoy chasing games, and spaniels retrieval games. When starting to play with a puppy, it is important to bear in mind the eventual size and temperament of the dog. Wrestling with a Rottweiler puppy will give that dog the message that it is OK to jump on people and roll around the floor with them! Not funny when the dog weighs 130 pounds (60 kg). There are two basic groups of games – those using the dog's instincts, such as chase and retrieve, and games using toys.

Playing Fetch

Dogs love games of fetch, but not all dogs will release the item when they have brought it back. This can be taught

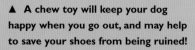

▲ A chew toy will keep your dog happy when you go out, and may help to save your shoes from being ruined!

▲ Dogs of all ages love a game of fetch, and it is a good game to include as part of your training sessions.

in a few simple steps. The first step is to teach the dog to hold an object. This should be something the owner chooses, otherwise the dog may bring back all sorts of things to the owner. The next step is for the dog to associate the command "Give!" or "Drop!" with the release of the item. Lots of praise and a tidbit when the dog reacts as required make the exercise a positive learning experience for the dog. The next stage is to encourage the dog to bring an item from a short distance away. Once the dog understands this, objects can be thrown for the dog to fetch. An extension of this is search games, where the dog has to seek out a toy or some food that the owner has hidden. Some dogs enjoy playing hide-and-seek with their owners.

Toys and Rules

Games with toys involve direct interaction and competition with the owner. They are therefore a wonderful chance to establish the relative roles of owner and dog without conflict. In games between dogs, the winner becomes number one in the hierarchy; therefore the owner must "win" every game with the dog, even if this means cheating! Play should always be initiated by the superior participant, the human, who should also keep possession of the toys, which are only brought out at playtime. The dog can have chews for amusement when alone. Games should not overexcite the dog, and play should be stopped at the earliest sign of this. In this way, dogs learn to play safely, and sooner or later can be played with by children. In a family, it helps if everyone plays with the dog by the same rules.

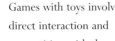

▲ **A game of tug-of-war between two dogs can be fun, and also teaches them essential socialization skills.**

▲ **Chasing and catching toys is great exercise for your dog, both physically and mentally.**

what if there's a cat in my new home?

A

A new dog must be taught to respect a cat and to leave it alone – for the safety of both animals. To allow the dog to become familiar with the cat safely, the cat can be placed in a crate that is raised off the floor, or the dog can be put in a house cage. The dog should be rewarded for not pestering the cat. Within a few days, dogs and cats usually settle down together, and many even become firm friends.

? *Why does your other dog growl at me?*

Many dogs find it hard to accept the arrival of another dog into the household. Another pet means sharing of territory, of owner's time and affection, and of toys. The initial introduction is best done in the yard. If the newcomer is a puppy, it will treat the older dog as if it were one of its own pack, by biting its ears and tugging its tail, in an attempt to initiate play. This can annoy the older dog, who will growl at the puppy to warn it off. If the growl fails to have the desired effect, a snap will follow. The senior dog will want to assert dominance over the newcomer, and to keep control of its bed, food, toys, and other resources.

In time, the majority of dogs settle into a good friendship. Introducing a puppy at the youngest possible age (about six weeks) will mean that the puppy is less apprehensive, and will settle down sooner.

Making Friends

However appealing your new dog, the old one still needs as much attention.

? Why must I wear a collar and leash?

Collars are essential for control and for carrying identity disks, so it is important that a dog learn to accept a collar, and the younger the dog, the easier it will be. Putting the collar on the dog for a short period at feeding time is a good way to introduce a dog to wearing a collar. Once it has accepted this, a leash can be attached. Again, this can be timed to coincide with meals, so that both the collar and the leash are associated with a pleasant experience. Walks around the yard on the leash can then begin, in preparation for the outside world. Early leash-training can mean happier, well-behaved walking later in life, especially as there are many areas, such as public parks, where dogs must be kept on a leash.

The rights of the older dog should be respected and protected by the owners, so that the newcomer is not permitted to run off with toys and food.

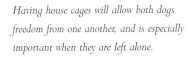

Having house cages will allow both dogs freedom from one another, and is especially important when they are left alone.

what's a puppy party?

A

After leaving the litter, it is important for puppies to continue to have contact with other dogs, and to learn to interact with them. Failure in this respect can produce a dog that is fearful of other dogs, and reacts by either running away or showing aggression. Puppy socialization parties are a response to this need. They are held at dog training centers or veterinary practices, and give puppies an opportunity to meet and communicate with other puppies and their owners, under supervision. Usually, a group of dogs under about four months of age attend a series of weekly parties. Useful advice and guidance is also given.

Here I Come!

The earlier socialization begins, the better adapted the dog will be.

Socialization involves the puppy's meeting lots of new people and other animals. To help the puppy become accustomed to noise and traffic, take it out of the house frequently.

? What does the word socialization mean?

Socialization is the process by which puppies become familiar with other animals and people. Puppies also need exposure to the environment in which they will live, such as traffic, cars, and noise. This should occur early in a puppy's life. There is a time known as the "sensitive period," from three to fourteen weeks of age, when a puppy can cope with these stimuli. A puppy deprived of such contact then will be generally fearful and will often show aggression throughout its life. By eight weeks of age, a puppy's response to something new is likely to be fearful, which is why some animal behaviorists now believe that the best time for a puppy to leave the litter and move to a new home is between six and eight weeks of age. Dogs with problems in later life are often those that have stayed with the breeder into or past the sensitive period, or those that are kept indoors by their new owners.

It can be helpful for the dog to receive a daily check of ears, feet, and teeth from its owner or a visitor. This accustoms the dog to being examined, so that visits to the veterinarian are less stressful, and the dog more manageable.

Why can't I go to the bathroom indoors?

A

Housebreaking, or the art of persuading a dog to relieve itself on grass rather than carpet, should be a relatively straightforward process. Newborn puppies are stimulated to urinate and defecate by their mother's licking the perineal area. The mother also cleans up after them. At about three weeks of age, when they are becoming more mobile, the puppies instinctively begin to leave the nest for this purpose. By eight weeks, they are moving farther from the nest, and starting to use predictable locations. This is when housebreaking can begin.

? How do I know where to go?

As puppies move away from the nest, they also begin using their sense of smell, sniffing the ground for scent markers before urinating. The owner can help by always taking the puppy to the same location, where it will pick up the scent of previous visits. The dog will soon adopt the habit of using the same spot. Once a scent has been left in the house, the dog is more likely to soil in that spot again. Cleaning with a biological detergent or an odor-eliminating enzymic cleaner is the best way to remove the scent. Dogs are unhappy about soiling the area where they eat and sleep, so if a dog is put in a small pen or cage, it is unlikely to dirty it unless desperate. However, it should not be left alone for too long. Dogs should never be punished for a lapse in housebreaking. This can inhibit the dog from relieving itself with the owner present, and lead it to soil secretly in another location.

Housebreaking

The basis of successful training is to provide the puppy with frequent opportunities to relieve itself in an appropriate place, and to reward it when it does perform there.

A puppy should be taken outside at specific times: after sleep, after meals, whenever it is let out of its pen, and every one to two hours. Always praise the puppy when it uses the correct place. An observant owner will gradually begin to spot the signs that indicate the dog's needs, such as sniffing and circling.

One method of training is to put newspaper on the floor, and reward the puppy when it uses the paper. Once this idea is established, the paper can be moved progressively nearer the door, and eventually outside. However, this method can delay housebreaking, since it permits the dog to soil indoors at first.

Once a dog is housebroken, you can also train it to eliminate on command. Just as the dog starts to perform, use a special command, such as "Be clean!" As soon as the dog has finished, give it a treat and lots of praise. The dog will soon associate the words with the activity.

What should my diet consist of

Can I have cat food instead of dog food

Why do some dogs get more food than others

I've put on some weight. Does it matter

SPECIAL FEATURE: A safe home

I love vegetables. Are they good for me

What would you feed me if I were sick

Why do you groom me so often

Why do I shed my hair

Yuck! Do you really have to clean my ears twice a week

These fleas really irritate. What can you do about them

Do I have to have my teeth cleaned

Daily Care

A dog needs a lot of care and commitment. It is not enough just to feed the dog once a day. Exercise, play, grooming, elimination of parasites, and the correct diet are all important aspects of dog care, and regular time spent caring for your dog will strengthen the bond between you.

A

Q. what should my diet consist of

Food is used by a dog for two reasons. First, nutrients are required for growth and to keep the body in good condition. Second, food is a source of energy. Energy is required for exercise and for many bodily functions, such as breathing, heartbeat, and maintenance of body temperature. Certain nutrients are essential to keep a dog healthy. These are proteins, fats, vitamins, minerals, and water.

Proteins are a vital constituent of all body cells, and are involved in metabolism and defense against disease. Fats contain some essential fatty acids. They also contain vitamins, and provide a source of energy. Vitamins are crucial to many metabolic pathways, although they are only required in tiny amounts. Many cannot be synthesized by the dog, and therefore have to be obtained from its diet. Minerals are also required, though again only in small quantities. They play some vital roles within the body; for example, calcium and phosphorus are an integral part of bones and teeth, and sodium and potassium are involved in cell metabolism and fluid balance.

Carbohydrate is not essential for dogs, but can be used as a source of energy. Carbohydrates come in three major forms: sugar, starch, and fiber or roughage. Sugar and starch are sources of energy.

Meal Options

A balanced diet for a dog will contain all the essential nutrients in the correct proportions.

Provided the dog receives a balanced diet, there is no reason why you should not mix different types of dog food; for example, dry food with a small amount of canned food added to make it more appealing. It is best not to feed a dog leftovers and table scraps, because this can lead to finicky eating habits and obesity.

? *I find this dry food so boring. Can I have anything with it?*

Nowadays, there is a large range of commercial canine foods available, both dry, semi-moist, and canned. Many are complete diets, containing all the essential nutrients in the correct amounts. Others are intended to be mixed, for example, canned food with dry food, and some dogs prefer this.

A premium dog food will be safe, free of bacteria and toxins. It will be specially formulated to meet a dog's nutritional and digestive needs at various stages in its life.

? can I have cat food instead of dog food **?**

A

Cats have a much higher protein requirement than dogs, so cat food is richer in protein. If a dog is fed cat food, the surplus protein that the dog cannot use is broken down into waste products for excretion. Some of these, such as urea, are potentially toxic. Urea is normally excreted into the urine by the kidneys. If a dog's kidney (renal) function is not fully effective, urea could accumulate in the body. Over a long period, excess protein in the dog's diet could contribute to the progression of kidney disease.

❓ *The dog next door gets vitamin and mineral tablets. Why don't I?*

Some owners prefer to feed their dogs fresh food. In the wild, dogs eat more than just the muscle meat from their prey. They also consume the skin, bones, and guts. As a result, they receive all the nutrients they need. Formulating a home-prepared diet needs careful consideration, and vitamin and mineral supplements can form an important part of such a diet. The advice of a veterinarian should be sought before giving a dog supplements.

❓ *Whenever I drink milk, I get diarrhea. Why is this?*

Cow's milk contains quite a lot of lactose, a milk sugar. Bitch's milk, on the other hand, contains little lactose. Newborn puppies can digest lactose, using an enzyme called lactase. As puppies get older, many lose this ability, and become intolerant to lactose. This intolerance causes diarrhea. Dogs vary in their reaction to milk, and their tolerance may alter with age.

Eggs can be a problem if fed raw. Raw egg white contains a substance known as avidin, which binds a vitamin named biotin, making it unavailable. Biotin plays an essential role in several metabolic processes. Deficiency can cause dry skin and hair loss. Cooking destroys avidin, so dogs can be given cooked eggs.

Food Dangers

Dogs fed a premium commercial food rarely need supplements, because these diets contain all the nutrients a dog needs.

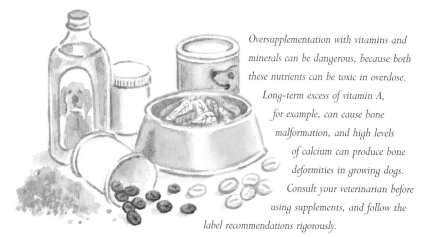

Oversupplementation with vitamins and minerals can be dangerous, because both these nutrients can be toxic in overdose. Long-term excess of vitamin A, for example, can cause bone malformation, and high levels of calcium can produce bone deformities in growing dogs. Consult your veterinarian before using supplements, and follow the label recommendations rigorously.

why do some dogs get more food than others?

A

The amount of food a dog needs is determined by its energy requirements, which depend on many factors, such as age, size, lifestyle, and ambient temperature. Excess food will be converted into fat. Insufficient food can result in poor growth in young dogs, and weight loss in older dogs.

Some dogs, such as small terrier breeds, are constantly active, and can eat quite a lot of food without gaining weight. Working dogs, such as collies, need much more food than pet dogs. Dogs that live outside need more energy than indoor pets to maintain their body temperature. Pregnant and lactating bitches also need more energy and more protein in their diet for puppy formation and milk production. Once the pups are weaned, their nutritional requirements will escalate as they grow and become more active.

Less energy is required by dogs who, for whatever reason, are less active. Some dogs are just plain lazy. Others may have some physical disability that makes exercise difficult, or have owners who never take them out. Older dogs need less food, as do those living in warm climates. Generally, females require less food than males, especially after they have been spayed.

? *I love chocolate. Why can't I have some?*

Chocolate contains a chemical called theobromine. This has to be metabolized and cleared by the liver. In humans, this takes about two hours. In dogs, it takes 18 hours, and requires a lot of work by the liver. Toxic levels of theobromine can soon build up, especially if the liver is not functioning well. Cocoa is the most dangerous form of chocolate for dogs, followed by dark and then milk chocolate.

Small dogs are at most risk. As little as 2 ounces (50 g) per 2 pounds (1 kg) of body weight can be lethal to pets that are sensitive to theobromine. This means that a small bar of chocolate could kill a Chihuahua. Not all dogs are sensitive, though, and many can safely eat some chocolate. It is fattening, however, so it should only be given in very small amounts. Chocolate treats especially manufactured to be safe for dogs are widely available, but should still only be given in small quantities.

The Correct Diet

It is important to balance a dog's diet according to its age, size, activity level, and general health status. Petfood manufacturers produce a fantastic range of foods to suit the needs of individual dogs.

Dogs with a high energy requirement will benefit from a concentrated diet, which will satisfy their needs without their having to consume vast quantities of food.

Some dogs need fewer calories than others. Such dogs can be given a "light" diet, which is especially formulated with less calories but still satisfies the dog's appetite.

There are many special diets available from veterinarians for dogs with specific clinical conditions, such as kidney or liver disease and bowel problems.

SPECIAL
FEATURE

A Safe Home

Sometimes dogs eat things that are not merely unhealthy but positively dangerous, and this can result in serious illness or even death.

There are hazards all around for our dogs – in our homes, yards, parks, and countryside. Some dogs are born scavengers, and cannot resist raiding a trash can or nosing in ditches, grabbing and eating anything that smells remotely appealing to them. Other dogs have dangerous habits, such as chewing sticks and stones and swallowing gravel. Sometimes it is the owner that gives the dog the dangerous item, such as a bone or

human medicine. Dogs most at risk are puppies – innocent, curious, and eager to put anything in their mouths.

Intestinal Obstruction

One of the most common problems seen in veterinary practice is intestinal obstruction. It can be caused by a huge variety of objects, such as children's toys, stones, corncobs, sticky tape, rubber balls, and bones. Bones can be hazardous. In addition to fracturing teeth, they can splinter and can become wedged in the throat,

▲ **All dogs love chewing on a tasty marrow bone, but you should take it away from the dog if it starts to break up or shatter.**

▲ **Special toys that a dog can chew are a safer option than giving your dog a bone.**

stomach, or gut. Sharp spikes can perforate the intestines, causing a fatal peritonitis. Surgery to remove the foreign body is major surgery, and sometimes involves a bowel resection if part of the gut wall has died. The bowels of dogs that have eaten bones much of their lives are often stuck together with scar tissue from the injuries caused by the bones.

Small bones and those that splinter easily, such as chicken bones, should never be given to dogs. Large, hard marrow bones may be safe, but must be taken away from the dog at the first sign of breaking.

Prevention of intestinal obstruction is far preferable to surgery, so dogs should be given safe playthings to chew, such as hard rubber toys of a suitable size for their breed.

Poisons

Poisons abound in every home. Potentially lethal substances include detergents, disinfectants, paint remover, and human medicines. The yard is no safer, with many households keeping a supply of toxic chemicals for killing weeds, rodents, and insects. There are also poisonous plants and fungi: laburnum, yew, daffodil bulbs, laurel leaves, and numerous berries, for example.

While many human drugs are used in veterinary medicine, there are many others that are unsafe for dogs. Even when human drugs can be given to a dog, the dose for a dog can be very different from that for a human. Therefore, a dog should never be given its owner's medicine, and in the case of accidental consumption, a veterinarian should be contacted immediately.

Signs of Trouble

Signs of intestinal obstruction include vomiting, diarrhea, loss of appetite, and pain lasting several days. The signs of poisoning are much more acute and vary tremendously, depending on the poison. Vomiting, weakness, convulsions, and collapse are just a few. A case of suspected poisoning must have veterinary help as soon as possible. There are few specific antidotes, and treatment is usually supportive and symptomatic. It is a great help to the veterinarian if the actual poison is known.

▲ Make sure your dog's toys are of a suitable size for its breed, and bear in mind that all toys will eventually wear out and should be replaced before they become a hazard.

▲ A young dog may be unwilling to give up a found plaything, so it is important to teach your dog to "Give!" or "Drop!"

I've put on some weight. Does it matter?

A

Obesity affects
over 30 percent of dogs
in developed countries. It
is a major health problem, and one usually
induced by the owners. Overweight dogs are at greater
risk of many health problems. The increased weight puts
strain on the body systems, contributing to diseases such as arthritis,
heart failure, bronchitis, and diabetes mellitus. Anesthetic risk is
greater in fat dogs. The layer of fat around the body has an
insulatory effect, causing the dog obvious distress in hot weather.
Fat dogs are unable to enjoy life as much as their slimmer friends,
and they tend to be reluctant to play and to go out. They prefer to
sleep, and may even refuse a short walk. They pant if they are
made to run, have difficulty going up steps, and tire easily.

Weightwatching

With the exception of a few metabolic causes, obesity in dogs is the result of overfeeding.

When calorie input exceeds energy needs, the excess is converted into fat. The easiest way to tell whether your dog is too fat is to run your hands along each side of its body, from head to tail. If fat can be felt on the dog's sides, around its neck, and at the base of its tail, the dog has a serious weight problem.

Some dogs are accomplished beggars, and can look very appealing. It gives people great pleasure to spoil their dogs and to share treats with them. Unfortunately, this is often how the weight creeps on, and because it is an insidious process, the owner may not realize what is happening.

? What is the best way to lose weight?

To lose weight, a dog needs fewer calories and more exercise. This can be achieved simply by feeding less food and fewer treats. A dog should never be put on a crash diet. One of the healthiest ways to reduce a dog's weight is to implement a reducing diet under veterinary supervision. These are special diets that are low in calories but contain fiber, so that the dog does not feel hungry. Treats can still be given, but they should be "healthy" ones, such as pieces of fruit and vegetable. Carrot is a favorite treat of many dogs, because it is sweet. Increasing exercise will also help a dog to lose weight, but it must be done gradually. A veterinarian can give advice on how to do this safely and on the best forms of exercise for an overweight dog.

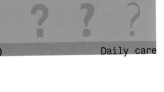

I love vegetables. Are they good for me?

A

Vegetables can be fed as part of a dog's meal, or used as treats. Both options are healthy, especially if the vegetables are fed raw or lightly cooked. They can provide tasty extra food for dogs on reducing diets, and are a good source of vitamins and minerals. Do not feed a dog potatoes, as these can cause diarrhea and flatulence.

? *Why do I eat grass?*

Dogs commonly eat small amounts of grass. Following this, they often vomit the grass along with some clear mucus. Otherwise, the grass is digested and passed in the feces. It would seem that dogs eat grass if their digestive tracts feel uncomfortable. Dogs with partial obstructions have been known to eat huge amounts of grass to induce vomiting, apparently in an attempt to shift the obstruction. If grass-eating is accompanied by loss of appetite, weight loss, and diarrhea, a veterinarian should be consulted. Otherwise, the occasional eating of grass is not harmful, provided the grass has not been sprayed with chemicals.

? *Why can't I sit down to lunch with you?*

Feeding a dog human meals can cause several problems. The diet may not contain everything a healthy dog needs, and may result in nutritional deficiencies, or overfeeding and obesity. Feeding such food can turn dogs into fussy eaters. They then refuse all but their favorite food, and train the owners to supply it! Dogs have been known to prefer Chinese food, cauliflower with cheese sauce, and spaghetti bolognese to their own food.

Table Manners

Dogs should be fed from their own bowl, containing their own food, after the rest of the family has eaten.

In the wild, dogs and wolves hunt in packs. After the kill, there is a hierarchical order of eating, with the leaders of the pack eating first. In the home situation, having a dog at the table with its owners, or eating at the same time, is placing the dog on an equal footing within the family pack. This can lead to dominance-related behavior problems.

Dogs should not be given scraps at human mealtimes, because this causes begging behavior and obesity. Success in demanding food from their owners can lead pet dogs into feeling quite dominant.

what would you feed me if I were sick?

A

Dogs that are sick or in pain frequently lose their appetites. This is often one of the first signs of ill health in dogs. Good nutrition can contribute greatly to their recovery, so tempting food should be provided. Sick dogs are best fed small amounts three to four times a day rather than one large meal. This is one situation where homemade food can really benefit a dog. A good intake of water is also important. A veterinarian may also prescribe electrolyte fluid to help avoid dehydration.

? *What should I eat if I've got diarrhea?*

Dogs with gastrointestinal upsets are best fasted for 24 hours. Fresh water should be available at all times, but if the dog is vomiting, it should only be supplied in small volumes. After a day's fasting, the dog can commence a bland diet, for example, plain cooked fish or chicken (with no added fat) and rice. This should be fed in three to four small meals a day, until the feces are normal. The return to a regular diet should be carried out gradually over several days, because sudden changes in diet can cause more diarrhea. Milk acts as a laxative, and should not be given. There are many causes of diarrhea in dogs. If it persists for more than two days or is accompanied by vomiting, a veterinarian should be consulted.

Convalescent Diets

Nicely cooked fresh food, served warm, will tempt the sickest of dogs to eat, especially if hand-fed by the owner. Small, frequent meals are better for the dog than one or two large meals.

Chicken and fish are preferable to red meat, which is harder to digest. Rice and pasta are good sources of carbohydrate.

❓ *What's all the fuss about? Just because I eat feces sometimes!*

Some dogs have the most disgusting habits. They seem to have an uncontrollable desire to eat revolting things, including feces. Eating feces is known as *coprophagia*. It is a common problem in dogs, and while occasionally it can be a sign of a physical disorder, it is usually a behavioral problem. The most obvious way to overcome it is to introduce an element that makes the feces taste vile. Feeding a dog pineapple or zucchini has this effect, as does putting menthol or eucalyptus on the feces. If none of these methods is effective, there are several other remedies that a veterinarian can recommend.

Water and electrolyte replacement may be very important. A sick dog should be offered small amounts of fresh water or electrolyte fluid every hour. If the dog is allowed to drink a large amount all at once, it may vomit. Dogs that won't drink may require intravenous fluids under veterinary supervision.

A

Q. why do you groom me so often?

A grooming session is more than just a brushing down. It is a time together that can enhance the relationship between dog and owner. In addition to getting the dog accustomed to being handled, it is an excellent opportunity to check thoroughly the dog's coat, skin, feet, eyes, ears, and teeth. Longhaired dogs often get twigs, leaves, and lumps of mud caught in their coat. Regular grooming removes loose hair and debris, and prevents matted sections from forming.

While that is being done, the skin beneath can be checked for signs of fleas, such as flea dirt. Lumps, bumps, and scabs that would otherwise go unnoticed can be detected. A buildup of grease and dirt in ungroomed fur can lead to skin irritation and blocked pores. Longhaired breeds can get dirty around the anal area. Breeds that need clipping or stripping should be professionally groomed every six to eight weeks.

? **Why do I feel so good after you have groomed me?**

Grooming aerates the coat and stimulates blood supply to the skin. This all contributes to a healthy coat. It also removes many of the dead hairs that are constantly being shed by almost all breeds. A healthy dog has a glossy coat with a sheen on it. The skin beneath should be clean, and pink or black. Dogs want to be cuddled and petted. It is difficult to do this lovingly with a dog that smells and has a matted coat. A well-groomed dog is happier, because it feels clean, admired, and desirable.

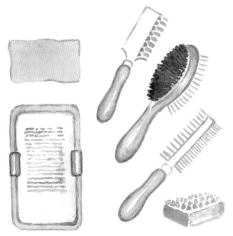

A Good Brushing

Most dogs love being groomed, especially if they are accustomed to it from puppyhood. It is a time when they have the owner's sole attention, and it can be a pleasant and relaxing exercise for both dog and owner.

There are several different types of grooming brush. Wire pin brushes are good for longhaired dogs, such as collies, and rubber brushes for shorthaired dogs, such as labradors. Thin-haired dogs need gentle brushing with a bristle brush.

Groom dogs from the back end toward the front (the opposite direction to stroking), and upward at the sides and chest. Tails are a sensitive area in some dogs, so take care when brushing this part. Finish each grooming session by brushing the coat in the direction the fur lies.

Some dogs, such as those with long or curly coats, need grooming frequently, while shorthaired dogs, such as boxers, need minimal coat care. Wirehaired breeds have harsh outer coats and thick, soft undercoats. In addition to brushing, these need stripping regularly to remove dead hair.

Q. Yuck! Do you really have to clean my ears

Dogs' ears come in a wonderful range of sizes and shapes, from the small pricked ears of terriers to the long pendulous ears of bloodhounds. They should be clean, not smelly, and clear of wax. The first part of the canal that leads to the eardrum runs parallel to the side of the head, before turning inward at about 70 degrees. This shape means that moisture and wax can accumulate in the canal.

This is a problem commonly found in dogs with hairy and pendulous ears. The ears tend to accumulate debris and moisture and have little air movement – ideal conditions for bacterial and fungal infections deep in the canal. Such ears need to be cleaned twice a week and kept as free of hairs as possible. A veterinarian or professional groomer can demonstrate how to clean dogs' ears. Any signs of infection, such as odor, redness, and inflammation, mean veterinary attention is needed. Besides infections, dogs can suffer from ear mites and foreign bodies, such as grass seeds.

? Why must I have my nails clipped?

Foot care is important, and should be carried out at least once a week. The weekly grooming session is a good time to do this. Nails can grow quickly, especially if the dog is not exercising on hard ground. Long claws are at risk of getting caught and pulled – a very painful experience. They can also curl over and dig into the pad. Nails can be clipped by a groomer, a veterinarian, or by the owner. At the same time, the nail beds can be examined for any signs of infection. The feet should also be checked for lumps of mud, foreign objects, and matted fur stuck between the pads. These are problems seen especially in dogs with hairy feet, such as Pekingese.

twice a week

Yuck! Do you really have to
clean my ears twice a week

? 47

Nail and Eye Care

Nails should be cut so that when the dog is standing, they are just in contact with the ground or a little above it. Eyes should also be cleaned regularly.

Dogs' claws contain an area of tissue with nerve and blood vessels, known as the quick. The length of the quick varies between individuals. It can be seen in white nails. This must be avoided, because it is painful when cut, and the bleeding is difficult to stop.

Unless these were removed in puppyhood, a dog may have dew claws. They are found on the inner part of the leg, above the foot, and are the equivalent of human thumbs. Dew claws also have nails that need trimming.

Eyes should be bright and clear, with no cloudiness, redness, or discharge. They can be gently cleaned with a damp cotton ball. Special eye cleaners are available, or plain water can be used.

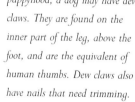

why do I shed my hair?

A

Except for a few breeds, all dogs shed. Hair growth and loss occurs in cycles, and while hair is growing or static in some follicles, it is falling out of others. These cycles are under the influence of various hormones. At certain times, such as spring, many dogs shed a great deal, as old hair from their thick winter coat is replaced. While most dogs shed a small amount of hair throughout the year, some shed excessively, and can make a lot of work for their owners. This is worse in breeds that originated in cold climates and are now kept indoors, especially in very warm homes. Occasionally, excessive shedding is caused by skin disease or hormonal problems.

? Should I have these bald patches?

Sometimes dogs shed so much hair at once that they develop areas of alopecia. There is always some underlying reason for this. The hair loss is most often caused by the dog biting and scratching itself because its skin is itchy. The itchiness is provoked by mites, fleas, or allergic reactions. The problem is exacerbated if the scratching introduces infection, which makes the dog even more itchy.

If not self-inflicted, hair loss may be caused by poor nutrition, stress, and debility affecting hair growth. A period of stress, such as lactation in a bitch with many puppies, or prolonged illness resulting in poor intake of nutrients, can cause a poor coat and hair loss. Hormone imbalance is another major cause; for example, overproduction of steroids by the adrenal glands, or an underactive thyroid gland. Many older dogs develop thin coats, but this is a normal aging change. In cases of abnormal alopecia, the hair is often lost from certain parts of the body, such as the flanks. A veterinarian will carry out tests on the skin and blood to diagnose the cause of the hair loss, which in most cases can be treated.

Fur Coats

A dog's coat provides warmth, insulation, protection, and waterproofing. Coats vary enormously between breeds, from short and thin through curly to long and thick.

Dogs have two different sorts of hair: primary guard hairs and secondary hairs. The primary hairs are relatively thick, coarse, and straight. The secondary hairs are thinner, wavy, and softer, and form an undercoat. The mix of primary and secondary hairs gives each particular breed of dog its characteristic coat texture. For example, Boxer and Doberman adults have only primary hairs, whereas Poodles have almost no primary hairs, only soft secondary ones.

The proportion of primary to secondary hairs is affected not only by breed, but also by the season of year and whether the dog lives in or outdoors; in winter, a dog will have more secondary hairs to keep it warm.

...These fleas really irritate.

Bathtime

Fleas running around on a dog and biting its skin will certainly irritate. However, the worst itchiness occurs when a dog is allergic to flea saliva. When fleas feed on an animal, they release a small amount of saliva, which contains several possible allergenic factors. Dogs that develop a flea allergy suffer extreme itching, and as a result, traumatize their skins, producing bald areas, raw sores, and skin infections. Areas most usually affected are the back, groin, and thighs. Live fleas may not be seen, but flea feces – small reddish-black comma-shaped dirt – can be found in infected dogs. Fleas also carry tapeworm, so flea control is a vital part of the dog's routine care.

There are many different insecticide treatments available. Look for a product that kills fleas on the dog, is easy to apply, and is effective for several weeks. Be sure the dosage is adjusted to the weight of your dog. Shampoos and collars tend to be ineffective, and many dogs hate sprays. Several preparations can be applied to one spot on the dog, from where they spread all over the skin and last for several weeks. Treatments must also be applied to the environment to eradicate the flea population there.

An occasional bath will help to keep a dog healthy and feeling good. If a dog is introduced to bathing when it is a puppy, it will usually grow up to enjoy bathtime, especially if it is rewarded with treats for good behavior.

What can you do about them

These fleas really irritate.
What can you do about them

?
51

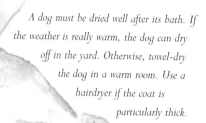

A good-quality canine shampoo and conditioner should be used if you bathe your dog more often than once every eight weeks. A vigorous massage with the shampoo stimulates the circulation to the skin, cleans the pores, and removes dirt and grease.

A dog must be dried well after its bath. If the weather is really warm, the dog can dry off in the yard. Otherwise, towel-dry the dog in a warm room. Use a hairdryer if the coat is particularly thick.

? *I smell great after I've rolled in cow muck, so why bathe me?*

Dogs find feces of all sorts very interesting. This is because they convey information about the animal that deposited the feces, such as species and sex. Dogs do not consider feces dirty and embarrassing as humans do. Rolling in them appears to be a reaction to the scent, and is normal canine behavior. However, it certainly does not render dogs attractive to their owners! Dogs also get smelly from swimming in dirty water and digging in the yard. So there are times when a dog must be bathed. Bathing removes a lot of dead hair, though a dog should always be groomed before a bath to remove tangles – unless, of course, it has just rolled in something disgusting.

A

From the day a dog's adult teeth erupt, plaque starts to accumulate on them. Plaque is a combination of food debris, bacteria, and saliva that adheres to the enamel of the teeth. In some dogs, if it is not removed daily, it continues to build up, becomes mineralized, and forms hard calculus. In time, this spreads down the tooth beneath the gumline, and acts as a trap for food debris and bacteria. Eventually, the gums become red, swollen, and sore. The combination of the calculus on the teeth and the inflammation of the gums (gingivitis) causes the teeth to loosen and eventually drop out.

The first sign of plaque and calculus on the teeth is often bad breath. The cure is a thorough clean-up by a veterinarian. However, prevention is better than cure. In the wild, dogs' teeth are cleaned by the food they consume – almost every bit of a carcass, and a good chew on the bones. Bones clean teeth, but they also fracture them. There are safer methods of keeping pets' teeth clean, and a daily dental hygiene routine should be followed.

Q. Do I have to have my teeth

Dental Hygiene

"Dog breath" is not a normal canine phenomenon. In the majority of cases it is caused by dirty teeth and gums. Dogs' teeth benefit from brushing, just as ours do.

cleaned ?

? Why don't I have fillings in my teeth?

Dental caries is rare in dogs. When they do occur, they affect the larger teeth at the back of the mouth. If decay is noticed early, a small filling procedure is feasible. However, by the time the caries lesion is discovered, it is usually so large and invasive that a filling would not be strong enough to withstand the demands put upon the tooth. It is better for the dog to have the tooth removed.

For dogs that really will not tolerate having their teeth brushed, there is a huge variety of gels and chews that help to remove plaque from the teeth. The abrasive action of dry food also helps.

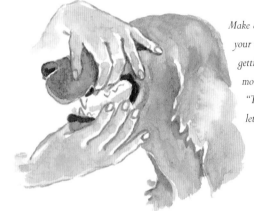

Make a toothbrushing session part of your dog's daily routine. Start by getting your dog used to having its mouth handled: lift the lip, say "Teeth!" and praise the dog for letting you do this.

Next, introduce some toothpaste — specially formulated products come in "doggy" flavors, such as poultry. Rub the paste onto your dog's teeth with your finger. Progress to using either a small, soft toothbrush or a plastic finger brush. The back molars need a lot of care, since these are most affected by calculus.

How do you know whether I am healthy

Why would you take my temperature

Why do I pant

Do we really need vaccinations every year

What does "neutering" mean

Why do I go into heat

SPECIAL FEATURE: Mating, pregnancy, and whelping

I can't stop drinking. Is this normal

What would you do if you saw me hit by a car

What would you do if I became lame

How would you know if I were in pain

What care would I need if I were very sick

Health Care

Health care is a major part of looking after your dog. Giving your dog a healthy lifestyle, appropriate vaccinations, and parasite control can prevent many health hazards. However, dogs still become sick and, of course, age. Recognizing problems, knowing how to deal with them, and consulting the veterinarian can enhance the length and quality of your dog's life.

How do you know whether I am healthy?

A

A healthy dog looks bright and alert. It should be interested in whatever is going on around it, and be responsive. The dog's coat should be glossy and feel good to touch. The dog should move easily, and appear content. A sick dog often looks dull and depressed, and has a drab, dry coat. It may move slowly, with body hunched and tail down.

? Why does the veterinarian ask about my eating, drinking, and bowel movements?

Loss of appetite and drinking very little or excessively are signs of ill health. A dog's excretory habits can also indicate a lot about its health status. Dogs normally defecate two or three times a day. The feces should be firm, with no blood or mucus present. However, there is much individual variation in both frequency and consistency, so owners should become aware of what is "normal" for their dog. This is also the case with urination – some dogs relieve themselves more frequently than others. Male dogs usually lift their legs to urinate; squatting may indicate a problem, such as arthritis.

? *Why is my nose wet?*

Most dogs have cool, wet noses when they are healthy. This is because there are many fluid-containing and mucus glands in a dog's nose, as well as two ducts that open into the area at the end of the nose. One is the naso-lacrimal duct, which carries tears from the eyes to the nose. The other carries fluid from the nasal gland specifically to keep the nose moist as a means of temperature regulation. When the moisture on the nose dries and evaporates, it lifts heat from the dog's skin. When a dog is overheated or has a high temperature, the nose becomes warm and dry.

Ears should not smell, and should not contain much wax. A dog with an ear problem will hold the affected ear down, shake its head, and sometimes scratch at the ear. Dogs can be afflicted by ear mites, infections, and foreign bodies, such as grass seeds, in their ears, all of which require veterinary attention.

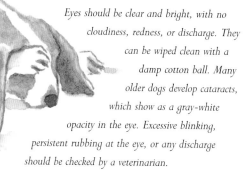

Eyes and Ears

These vital sense organs should be checked regularly and kept clean.

Eyes should be clear and bright, with no cloudiness, redness, or discharge. They can be wiped clean with a damp cotton ball. Many older dogs develop cataracts, which show as a gray-white opacity in the eye. Excessive blinking, persistent rubbing at the eye, or any discharge should be checked by a veterinarian.

A

The normal range for a dog's temperature is 100.4–102.0°F (38.0–38.9°C). Smaller, more active dogs tend to have temperatures at the upper end of this range. An elevated temperature is called pyrexia and occurs for many reasons, the most usual being some form of infection. Dogs with pyrexia have warm, dry noses and often drink more. If there is any sign that a dog is sick, it is worth checking its temperature.

? *What about my pulse?*

The normal pulse rate for a dog ranges from 70 to 160 beats per minute, depending on the size, age, and fitness level of the dog. Small dogs tend to have much higher heart rates than large breeds, and young dogs have faster pulses than adults. The pulse rate is raised with excitement, fear, pyrexia, hemorrhage, and certain heart conditions.

...why would you take my

? *How would you know if I had breathing problems?*

A dog's respiratory rate is between 10 and 30 breaths per minute at rest. The chest moves in and out in a rhythmic manner. Dogs with respiratory distress breathe much more rapidly, and may involve their abdominal muscles, so that breathing appears to be an effort.

temperature ?

Temperature, Pulse, and Respiration

Knowing how to check these values can be useful in assessing your dog's condition and reporting to the veterinarian.

? *Why does the veterinarian look at my gums?*

Gums are pink or black, depending on a dog's pigmentation. Only pink gums can offer useful indications to the veterinarian. Other mucus membranes that can help are the conjunctiva of the eye. Mucus membranes should be pink. Pallor of them suggests anemia, blood loss, or shock. Blueness indicates poor oxygenation of the blood, as in heart or chest conditions.

A dog's temperature is normally taken in the rectum. Lubricate the thermometer with petroleum jelly (do not use lubricants containing medicines or antiseptics, which may sting the delicate mucosa), and insert it a short way into your dog's anus. There are different sorts of thermometer available — the easiest to use are the electronic ones.

A dog's pulse should be palpable in the inner thigh. Your veterinarian will show you where to locate it. Count for 30 seconds, then double this number to obtain the rate per minute.

Respirations can also be counted for 30 seconds and doubled. One respiration equals an in and an out chest movement. Both respiration and pulse should be taken while the dog is sitting or lying quietly.

? why do I pant A

Panting is a rapid in-and-out breathing, with the mouth open and the tongue hanging out. The purpose of panting is to cool the dog down, and it is the only efficient way that dogs have of losing heat. The surfaces of the nose and mouth are kept moist, and as air passes over these surfaces, it takes up moisture and with it, heat. By panting rapidly and hanging the tongue out, the rate of heat loss is increased.

? Why do my pads sweat when I'm hot?

Dogs' pads contain sweat glands. Although a dog has sweat glands elsewhere, these are nearly all covered by hair, so the pads are the only parts that are clearly seen to sweat. They play a minor role in heat loss.

Hot Dogs

Because dogs have relatively little cooling ability, they can quickly succumb to heatstroke if left in a hot environment. This can be fatal.

Never leave your dog in a car or closed room on a hot day, or tie it up without access to shade and water. In hot weather, it is essential that a dog can move to a cooler location, and have water available to replace that lost by panting. It also needs ventilation, preferably through the movement of air.

? What makes my bottom itch?

On each side of a dog's anus, positioned at approximately 4 and 8 o'clock, are the two anal sacs. Each has a duct that opens just inside the anus. As the dog defecates, the anal muscles contract against the anal sacs, and secretions are squeezed out. In some dogs, this mechanism works inefficiently, with the result that the sacs become full. This is uncomfortable, and the dog licks its bottom and drags it along the ground (a behavior known as scooting). The anal sacs can be emptied by a veterinarian, and this should be done regularly, if necessary. Overfull glands can lead to infection.

Signs of heatstroke include rapid panting, distress, profuse salivation, bright red lips and tongue, and collapse. Immediate treatment is necessary to save life. The hot dog should be moved to a cooler place, and wetted thoroughly with wet towels or a shower. The dog can even be placed in a pool or a tub of cold water, but only for a couple of minutes at a time, otherwise chilling may occur. Veterinary help may be needed.

Do we really need vaccinations every year

A Immunity, or resistance to disease, is the role of the body's immune system, and is effected via certain proteins known as antibodies. Immunity to some diseases is passed from the dam to her puppies in her milk. However, this immunity only lasts a few weeks. After that, immunity can be gained in two ways: exposure to a disease or vaccination. Exposure to a disease usually produces lifelong resistance to it, *if* the dog survives – many don't. Vaccines work by stimulating a body to produce its own defense against disease, without the risk associated with actually catching the disease. However, the immunity that vaccines stimulate is not as long-lasting as that produced by the natural infection, and therefore regular boosters are advisable to keep a dog fully protected.

Clean Up

In addition to harming the health of the dog, some worms can also infect humans. Children are most at risk.

? What are parasites?

Parasites are organisms that live in or on another living organism. Those that live on the outside of an animal are termed ectoparasites, and a prime example in dogs is fleas. Mites and ticks are other ectoparasites that affect dogs. Internal parasites, known as endoparasites, principally inhabit the intestines, although there are also worms that live in the lungs, blood cells, and hearts of dogs. Others can migrate out of the intestines into muscle, liver, and brain. Endoparasites can seriously affect the health of a dog, or even kill it.

Most worms that infect dogs produce eggs, which are voided from the dog's body in its feces. Cleaning up after your dog is, therefore, an important health matter as well as a social one. Most urban and many other areas have laws regarding cleaning up after our dogs. To protect children from infection, and to prevent adverse publicity for dogs, we must clean up after our pets in public places. Our own yards must also be kept clean.

? Can you keep me from getting worms?

There are many excellent antiparasitic drugs. Some kill the adult parasites, some the larval stages. Most have few side effects for the dog. It is advisable to discuss the use of "wormers" with a veterinarian, who may send fecal samples for laboratory examination before prescribing a suitable antiparasitic drug.

Always wash your hands after cleaning up after your dog, and also after handling or stroking your dog. Don't let dogs lick faces.

Train your dog to soil in just one part of the yard, so that the rest is clean.

? what does "neutering" mean?

A Neutering involves removal of the reproductive organs. In female dogs the operation is referred to as spaying. When a bitch is spayed, the uterus and both ovaries are removed, so that she is then unable to become pregnant. Removal of the ovaries also stops her having periods of heat and false pregnancies. Neutering of a male dog involves the removal of both testicles.

? *Sounds painful. Is it?*

Spaying is major abdominal surgery, and the bitch will be sore for a day or two after the operation. Analgesic injection is usually given at the time of surgery, and postoperative pain relief can be supplied in tablet form, if necessary. The main risk is hemorrhage – although the major arteries are tied off during the operation, there are many small blood vessels in the tissues around the uterus that may ooze.

Neutering a dog is a simpler procedure. An incision is made just in front of the scrotum, and the testicles are removed through it. The scrotum is left in place, and shrinks over the subsequent few weeks. The dog is sore for a couple of days.

To Spay or Not to Spay?

Although spaying is major surgery and not without risks, it does prevent many potential health problems in later life.

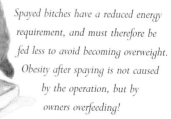

The advantages of being spayed include no heats, no false pregnancies, no risk of pyometra, and less chance of developing mammary tumors.

? Why do it?

The reasons for spaying include prevention of unwanted pregnancy and recurrent false pregnancies. Many bitches become quite moody during their heat cycle, and for several weeks afterwards. A major health problem in older females is a condition known as pyometra, when an infection builds up in the uterus. This life-threatening condition necessitates spaying, which is then a very risky procedure because of the accompanying toxicity. A bitch that was spayed when young and fit cannot get pyometra. The usual reasons for neutering a male dog are aggressive or dominant behavior, and inappropriate sexual behavior. A neutered dog cannot get testicular tumors, and is much less apt to develop tumors around the anus or prostate gland problems. And, of course, it cannot sire unwanted puppies.

The main risks from the operation are anesthetic death, hemorrhage, and infection. In later years, a spayed bitch may suffer a degree of urinary incontinence. However, this is easily treated with daily medication.

Spayed bitches have a reduced energy requirement, and must therefore be fed less to avoid becoming overweight. Obesity after spaying is not caused by the operation, but by owners overfeeding!

A

Every six months or so (in some breeds only once a year), a female dog comes into heat. This is her estrus cycle, when she becomes fertile and attractive to male dogs. The estrus cycle starts with a reddening and enlargement of the vulva, soon followed by a thin bloody discharge from the genital tract. The discharge becomes a straw-colored fluid, and pheromones produced in the urine and vulva draw the attention of male dogs, sometimes from miles around. The female herself seeks dogs and displays receptive behavior.

This is the only time when a bitch will accept a male, and this is when she can become pregnant. The entire cycle is under hormonal influence, and following ovulation, progesterone levels rise for several weeks. At this stage, the bitch is either pregnant or in a state of false pregnancy. After that, hormone levels fall, and all becomes quiet until the next heat.

why do I go into heat?

False Pregnancy

This occurs one to two months after a heat. The bitch shows signs of pregnancy and lactation, but produces no puppies.

False pregnancy is a normal physiological state for a female dog, and only some bitches show overt signs of it. These include making nests, adopting surrogate puppies, such as soft toys, and producing milk. Some become very restless and nervous, and may even go into a false labor.

Severe false pregnancies can be treated with drugs, such as hormones and sedatives. However, a bitch can be helped through milder ones, by taking away all the objects that she adopts, dismantling any nests, and giving her more exercise.

Some bitches undergo temperament changes at this time, so care should be taken if children are around.

? How likely am I to get mammary tumors?

Mammary tumors are fairly common in older, nonspayed bitches, and can be either benign or malignant. Malignant tumors are likely to spread to the lungs. The incidence of mammary tumors in spayed females is much lower, and the earlier the bitch is spayed, the less the risk. The incidence in dogs spayed before their first heat is less than 1 percent, compared with over 25 percent in bitches spayed after two or more heats. Early detection and removal of tumors is important, so monthly checks of the dog's mammary glands should be carried out.

? Can heats be prevented without spaying?

Heats can be prevented by the use of hormone injections or tablets. However, these treatments are not without risk and most veterinarians frown upon their use. Many people consider that spaying is the safest long-term option. If a bitch has an unplanned mating, hormones can be used to prevent the fertilized egg from implanting in the uterus.

Mating, Pregnancy, and Whelping

Mating can only occur if the bitch is receptive to the dog, which only happens when she is in full heat.

To mate, the dog mounts the bitch, wrapping his forelegs around her body, and inserts his penis into her vagina. After some thrusting, the dog then turns through 180 degrees, so that the dogs are bottom to bottom. Part of the penis swells and the vagina constricts around it, "tying" the dogs together. The "tie" can last for 5 to 50 minutes, but is not essential for pregnancy to occur. The most fertile time for a bitch is usually 10 to 14 days from the start of her heat. If pregnancy is desired, two matings 48 hours apart increase the chances of success.

Pregnancy

Pregnancy lasts an average of 63 days from the date of mating. It can appear to be much longer or shorter than this (a range of 54–72 days has been reported), because sperm can survive in the bitch's reproductive tract for several days before fertilizing eggs. Following a successful mating, it is many days before the fertilized eggs implant in the uterus and start to grow, so confirmation of pregnancy is best made at 28–35 days. This can be done by blood test,

▲ A bitch needs to be in full heat to be receptive to the dog. This young female is unsure about the playful attention of the dog.

▲ This female is heavily pregnant and will soon give birth. She will probably become restless and start building a nest.

ultrasound scan, or abdominal palpation by a veterinarian. From around 42 days, the puppy skeletons will show on radiographs.

Caring for a Pregnant Bitch

Although many exciting developments are taking place within her, the female dog shows little outward sign of change during the first weeks of her pregnancy. She may become more affectionate and "clingy." From the fifth week, the mammary glands enlarge, and the teats become redder. Abdominal enlargement is obvious by the seventh week. The pregnant bitch should receive a premium diet, and the amount fed should be slowly increased from week five.

As her uterus enlarges, she will find it easier to digest three to four small meals a day instead of one large one. No mineral supplements are necessary if she is receiving a good diet. She will drink more water, and need to urinate more frequently as the uterus presses on her bladder. Exercise can continue as before, with shorter walks in late pregnancy. Worming, under veterinary supervision, is very important. During pregnancy, some worms that are normally quiescent in muscle become active, and the larvae can cross the placenta to the pups.

Whelping

This is the delivery of the puppies. The bitch may well choose where she is going to give birth, but it must be a quiet and warm place, with plenty of clean bedding. In the last few days before whelping, the bitch becomes restless and may start to make "nests." When her body temperature drops and milk appears in the mammary glands, the pups will be born in the next 24 hours. She may have from one to twelve pups. Most litters comprise four to eight. Puppies are born at intervals of 30 minutes to two hours, and emerge still wrapped in the sac of fetal membranes. As soon as each puppy is born, the mother normally breaks open the sac, and chews through the umbilical cord that attaches puppy to placenta. Human intervention is sometimes required here. Occasionally the bitch is unable to produce the pups herself, and a Caesarean section is necessary.

▲ **Six contented puppies enjoy their first meal, while their mother takes the opportunity to rest.**

▲ **One of the newborn puppies fast asleep after an exhausting day.**

Q ... I can't stop drinking. Is

A

Water is essential for many of the body's metabolic processes, and water balance is carefully regulated by the brain, kidneys, and various hormones. A dog requires approximately 2 fluid ounces (50 ml) of water per 2 pounds (1 kg) of body weight in a 24-hour period. Some of this will be taken in the form of food, especially if the dog is fed on canned food. The rest is drunk.

Excessive drinking, polydipsia, is a sign of some disorder. It may be kidney disease, or a problem affecting the production of the hormones involved in water balance. Alternatively, the dog may be drinking a lot to compensate for increased urination, such as occurs with diabetes. Any change in drinking habits that continues for more than a day or two ought to be investigated. The veterinarian will need a urine sample.

? *The dog next door has an awful cough. Am I likely to catch anything?*

There are several causes of coughing in dogs, of which the most contagious is infectious laryngo-tracheitis, generally known as kennel cough. This is caused by a combination of organisms, and is easily spread from dog to dog. Vaccination provides partial protection. Other diseases that produce a cough include bronchitis, pneumonia, lung tumors, heartworm, and lungworm. Most dogs with heart disease develop a cough, which is often worse with exercise, or when the dog is lying down.

this normal

? I've been vomiting all day. Is it serious?

The usual reason for vomiting in dogs is dietary indiscretion, that is, eating something inappropriate. This could be bad food to which the stomach reacts, or an obstructive item, such as a bone. Vomiting is one of the main signs of intestinal obstruction. Some infectious diseases affect the gastrointestinal tract, and in such cases, vomiting is often accompanied by diarrhea. If either persists for more than 24 hours, veterinary advice should be sought, as dehydration can soon be a problem. Poisoning, motion sickness, and organ failure are just some of the many other causes of vomiting.

Signs of heart failure include panting and coughing. The coughing is worse with exercise, or when the dog is lying down, for example, at night. The dog becomes unable to exercise for long, and may be reluctant to go out for walks or to play.

Heart Failure

This is a common problem, especially in older dogs and certain breeds. It is often the result of valvular disease.

There is no cure for the condition, but there are medications to prolong the life of a dog with heart failure. A special diet may be recommended by your veterinarian.

At home, the most important aspect of care is keeping the dog slim. Extra weight means extra work for the heart. Exercise should be in small amounts on a regular basis, and because the dog is exercising less, it will need less food. Overexcitement should be avoided if possible.

? What would you do if you saw me hit by a car

A

Unless in immediate danger of additional trauma, the dog should not be moved until its injuries have been assessed. Look for signs of obvious injuries, such as bleeding and fractured limbs. Assess how conscious and alert the dog is. Observe its breathing, and check the color of its mucous membranes – a shocked dog will be very pale. The dog's airway may become blocked by its tongue or vomit – clear this if necessary. It is important to keep the dog warm, and get it to veterinary care as soon as possible. The utmost care should be taken when moving the dog, bearing in mind the nature of its injuries and the possibility of an aggressive reaction.

? What if I cut my pad badly?

A dog's pad often bleeds profusely when cut, because it has a rich blood supply. The carpal pad, which is slightly up the foreleg, is close to an artery, which must be ligated if cut to stop the bleeding. First-aid treatment of cut pads should be aimed primarily at stopping the bleeding, and involves pressing a pad of cotton or gauze over the cut. This should be bandaged firmly in place. If possible, a quick wash in a saline solution to remove loose dirt before applying the dressing is a good idea. If the blood comes through that dressing, another one should be added, increasing the pressure. Only a veterinarian should remove the dressing, in case the cut starts to bleed again. All such cuts should be examined by a veterinarian, because they may need stitching and treatment with antibiotics.

*Injured dogs should be restrained with a leash to
prevent them from running away. Because they
are frightened, and possibly suffering from
concussion, they may act out of character and
bite. Make a muzzle of some sort to place
around the dog's nose to protect yourself when
examining a strange casualty, but be careful not to
obstruct its breathing.*

Don't Panic

**Injured or convulsing dogs need reassuring, calm care.
If people around them panic, the dogs will also.**

? Suppose you found me having a convulsion?

A convulsion can be frightening to witness. The dog may
lose consciousness, froth at the mouth, and pass urine.
Convulsions usually last from 30 seconds to two minutes.
In this time, the dog should be kept in a quiet, dim area
with the drapes closed, the television turned off, and
everyone kept away from the dog except the person
looking after it. It is important to check that the dog
cannot hurt itself by falling downstairs or into an open fire.
On recovery, the dog will be disoriented and fearful, and
may bite, so it is important to keep it quiet and reassured
until fully recovered.

*Keep all people who are upset and noisy
away from the dog,
which will be affected
by their distress. Cover
the dog in a towel,
blanket, or coat for
warmth, and use it to
carry the dog to the
veterinarian's office.*

*Never give an injured dog anything
to eat or drink. It may need an
emergency anesthetic. Alcohol, in particular, can
cause a fall in blood pressure.*

A

Q. What would you do if I became

Lameness means that a dog is not using one or more of its legs fully, and this indicates pain. A dog may be 100 percent lame, that is, not using the leg at all, or just slightly lame. It may be more lame after rest or after exercise, depending on the cause of the lameness. There are many reasons for a dog to be lame, ranging from acute trauma, such as a sore foot, joint sprain, ligament tear, or fracture, to a chronic problem, such as arthritis or a slipped disk. Sometimes, the trauma responsible for the lameness has been witnessed, but in most cases the cause is not obvious.

The first question to ask is whether it is an acute problem, or whether it has become progressively worse over several weeks. If acute, check the foot for splinters, stones, torn nails, or cuts. If there is nothing to be seen, either consult with a veterinarian or let the dog rest for 48 hours, depending on how bad the lameness is. Lameness that is severe or does not improve with rest warrants a veterinary consultation.

lame

Stiff Dogs

Many dogs develop arthritis, as a result of trauma, a developmental abnormality, such as hip dysplasia, or just old age. Correct management of these dogs can make sure they have a comfortable life.

Pain relief in the form of nonsteroidal drugs is available, and there are many herbal and homeopathic remedies that may help.

Dogs with arthritis must be kept slim, so that their joints have less weight to bear. Exercise needs to be regular. It is best to have one or two short walks every day, rather than one long one on weekends. Swimming is a good form of exercise, but not in extremely cold water.

❓ *I itch badly every summer. Why?*

Itching in the summer can be so severe that dogs scratch themselves and chew their feet until they're sore. There are two main causes: mites and allergies. As in humans, dogs' allergies give rise to itchy skin in areas such as the feet, face, and limbs. An affected dog bites, chews, and licks at itself, and there is almost always a secondary skin infection present, which causes additional itching. Ears are often involved, and become chronically infected. There is hair loss from the affected areas, redness, and often small red spots. The many allergens to which dogs can become hypersensitive include flea saliva, house dust mites, pollens, and certain foods. Diagnosis of allergic skin disease is usually made by eliminating all other possible causes of the itching and infected skin. Skin tests are available to identify the precise allergens. Because fleas and pollens are more plentiful in warm weather, allergic skin disease is often worse in the summer months.

A soft, warm, draft-free bed keeps a dog comfortable.

Q. How would you know if I were in pain?

A

Dogs, like humans, can suffer both acute and chronic pain, but unlike humans, they cannot complain or take a tablet. It is therefore important that owners learn to recognize signs of pain in their dogs. Dogs in acute pain may pant and shiver, and be generally restless. Some may also growl and show aggression when being examined, while others become quiet and withdrawn. In dogs with chronic pain, the signs will be much more subtle. The dog may be stiff and reluctant to move, or restless and unable to settle. This sort of pain can make a dog depressed and lethargic. In fact, change of behavior and demeanor may be the only signs of chronic pain.

Tablet Time

The surest way to give tablets to a dog is directly into its mouth. Many dogs get very clever at detecting tablets in their food and ejecting them.

? Why can't I have your medicines?

There are many wonderful drugs for human use, and some of these are used by veterinarians to treat dogs. However, some human drugs are positively dangerous to dogs, who are unable to metabolize them. With others, the dosage for dogs is very different from that for humans, so dogs should never be given human medication without checking with the veterinarian first.

? What can I have for pain?

There are many painkillers specially formulated for dogs, in the group of drugs known as nonsteroidal antiinflammatories. These are relatively safe, even for long-term use. Possible side effects include gastric irritation and ulceration and renal damage. For acute pain, a dog may be given something stronger by the veterinarian, such as a morphine-type compound. Aspirin can be given to most dogs for a day or two, but always ask a veterinarian for advice before giving a dog pain medication.

Place one hand over the dog's muzzle, with your fingers pressing the lips inward just in front of the large carnassial teeth of the upper jaw. Use a finger of your other hand to open the dog's mouth, by pulling down on the front teeth (incisors).

The tablet should already be in this hand, and as the dog's mouth opens, put your hand in all the way to the back, depositing the tablet as far back as possible.

Hold the dog's mouth closed, and stroke its throat to stimulate swallowing. It is best to accustom your dog to this procedure as a puppy, by using soft treats.

Q. what care would I need if I were

A

For some dogs, care at home is preferable to being hospitalized, especially if the owners have the necessary time and skills. A sick dog will not move much, so frequent change of body position is important – it prevents pressure sores occurring over bony areas, and helps to prevent accumulation of fluid, and pneumonia, in the lungs. The dog may soil its bed. If this happens, clean it up well, and dry the dog's fur thoroughly, both for its comfort and to prevent sores. Fresh water should be offered every hour, and syringe feeding may be necessary. Food should be warm and tempting. Additional warmth may be necessary, since lack of movement may cause the dog to become chilled. A heat pad, heat lamp, or well-insulated hot water bottle can be used.

? *Do older dogs have special problems?*

Pet dogs are living longer now than ever before, and a number of age-related problems occur as various parts of their bodies begin to deteriorate. Some older dogs become partially blind, often because of cataracts, and deaf. Many also have arthritis in one or several joints, making movement difficult and slow. Their digestive systems cannot cope with large amounts of food or anything rich. Organs, such as the liver and kidneys, start to fail, and teeth become dirty, causing gingivitis. Tumors are common, some more serious than others.

Check regularly for abnormal lumps and bumps, and watch for any signs that may indicate pain.

very sick !

? *Are there any treatments?*

Surgery is available for tumors, tooth care, and cataracts, and modern drugs make anesthetics less risky than they were. Pain relief can be given for arthritis. As always, prevention is better than cure, and taking the dog to the veterinarian for a checkup every six months will mean that problems are detected early. Observations at home are also of great value; for example, water consumption, stomach upsets, and general demeanor.

The Older Dog

Older dogs have a mellowness and wisdom lacking in younger ones. They are very special, and should be treated with love and respect, and their lives made as comfortable as possible.

Give older dogs regular exercise, but don't expect them to manage long walks. Feed two small meals a day rather than one large one, and keep the dog's weight down. With less activity, it will need fewer calories.

Understand that the dog needs to relieve itself more frequently, and plan for this to prevent accidents. An older dog is less able to cope with extremes of temperature, so keep it warm in winter and out of the heat in summer.

Understanding your Dog

4

A thorough understanding of your dog — how it communicates, what makes it happy and unhappy, why it behaves in certain ways — will make the relationship between you and your dog strong. It also allows you to train your dog in a rational and fair way, resulting in a dog that is well-behaved and well-balanced.

A Q. Why is smell so important to me?

From the moment puppies are born, smell is their most important sense. Puppies are born blind and deaf – their eyes open at 10–14 days, and their hearing develops by 3–4 weeks of age. They locate their mother and the milk they need purely by smell, and this remains their most useful sense for the rest of their lives. Dogs' sight is not as accurate as that of humans. Some dogs are born with relatively poor eyesight, and others' sight deteriorates with age. All these dogs cope very well, using their nose and ears.

Scent gives a dog much general information. It is normal canine behavior to investigate anything new – whether it be an object, a human, or another animal – by sniffing at it enthusiastically. The smells from dogs' urine, feces, anal glands, vaginas, and scent glands around the neck and bottom give dogs lots of information about one another, which is why dogs spend so much time sniffing at rear ends on meeting. Dogs' acute olfactory senses are often put to use in tasks such as bomb and drug detection.

? Why do I urinate when I smell other dogs' urine?

As well as a source of general information, scent is an important means of communication between dogs, and both urination and defecation are used for this. In the wild, male dogs and wolves urinate in prominent places to scent mark the boundaries of their territory. Urine scenting is also related to sexual behavior – the scent left by a bitch in heat will inform dogs of her availability. Pet dogs urinate on street lamps, trees, seats, other animals' feces, and all other places where they detect the smell of other dogs. This marks what they may think of as their territory, tells other dogs of their presence, and masks previous scents.

Normal Behavior

While urine marking is normal behavior, it is not acceptable if done to excess or in the home.

Don't allow your dog to lift its leg every two minutes during a walk. This can ruin the walk, and mean the dog gets little exercise. After the first couple of stops, walk briskly past all likely objects, calling your dog to heel, and urging it on if it shows signs of stopping. Distraction with a treat or favorite toy may help.

Urinating in the house may be a territorial or dominance problem if there is more than one dog in the home. Sometimes submissive dogs wet at home if they feel insecure. In both these situations, the entire problem needs addressing, not just the urinating.

A dog's attachment to something that smells good can be useful if a dog becomes distressed when separated from its owner. The dog can be left with an item of the owner's clothing, which will bring comfort.

? I have to growl at other dogs to keep them from

A A growl from a dog can mean several things. It is usually a warning, meaning "Leave me alone," and often indicates anxiety about a situation. It may be disciplinary – pack leaders keep younger dogs under control by looks and growls before they ever need to nip them. The usual reason a dog on a leash growls at another dog is fear. A dog off the leash has the potential to escape or fight if it is worried by another dog. A dog on a leash does not have these options, and if feeling frightened, may adopt a policy of aggression in order to scare the other dog away. From the dog's point of view, this seems to work, because the other dog usually moves away or the owner removes the fearful dog.

? *Why do you stop playing with me when I growl?*

A dog growling in play may simply be playful. It is important to differentiate this sort of growl from a more dominant one. If a dog wins a game with its owner that involved growling, it can soon associate growling with winning, that is, getting what it wants. This can extend to other situations; for example, the dog that growls when the owner attempts to move it off the couch. Many owners become frightened by their dogs' growling, and in turn, the dogs become increasingly successful at getting their own way.

attacking me, don't I?

To help overcome the problem, the dog needs gentle and repeated exposure to the thing that it fears, combined with a good experience, such as receiving a treat from visitors or much praise when it doesn't bark at another dog. Fear aggression can take a lot of time and patience to overcome.

Fear Aggression

Many dogs showing aggression are actually frightened, and are simply trying to make the object of their fear, such as another dog or a visitor, go away.

A dog should never be shouted at or hit when showing fear aggression. This would only make the problem worse. Nor should the dog be reassured, because this could appear to be praising it for the behavior.

Remain calm and relaxed. This will convey itself to the dog, whereas anxiety on your part will only worsen the situation.

Why do I howl when left alone?

A Some dogs become very unhappy when left alone. They want to be reunited with other members of their pack. So, initially, they bark as if to say, "I'm here, folks, please come back." If that doesn't work, they bark a little louder. When that fails, they start to howl. Howling is a dog-to-dog distress call: "I'm about to be eaten by a wolf – come back NOW!" It is usually during this stage that the owners return, so the dog may conclude that its howls brought them back.

? *I'm barking to tell you there's someone at the door. Why do you scold me?*

A dog that barks whenever someone approaches the house can be a useful announcer of visitors and a burglar deterrent. However, a dog that continues to bark can be extremely annoying, both to its owners and their neighbors. Dogs see people that come to the house as potential intruders, and may feel frightened of them. They bark to scare these "intruders" away, and in many cases it works, because the mail carrier, for example, has no intention of staying anyway!

Be Quiet!

It is normal for dogs to bark. However, persistent barking is unacceptable, and dogs can be trained out of it.

? *Are there any other reasons I bark?*

A bark can mean many things. It may be a greeting to a special human. It may be a request to play, or an attention-seeking device. Dogs bark to threaten other animals and people, or to call for company if left alone. Sometimes, the barking is appropriate and acceptable; other times, it is not. Barking for attention is often very successful. The natural reaction is to tell the dog to be quiet, or distract it with toys or even food.

Do not shout at your dog in an attempt to control the barking — it will think you are joining in and will bark even more! When your dog is barking, ignore it. Do not stroke or talk to it, since this will be misconstrued as praise.

To teach a dog to be quiet, you must first teach it to bark on command. This can be done by stimulating it to bark. Use whatever it would normally bark for, such as its food or a ball. As soon as your dog starts to bark, give a command word, such as "Bark!" and reward it. Keep the dog barking for several seconds, if possible. When it takes the reward, it has to stop barking, because its mouth will be otherwise occupied.

Having established barking to order, you can teach the "Quiet!" command. When the dog has been barking for several seconds, pretend you are about to reward it. As it goes quiet to take its treat, say the word "Quiet!" and reward it. Practice makes perfect, but the timing in this training exercise is crucial.

Q. I accept my human family as my pack.

A

Dogs are pack animals. The pack gives them support and protection. The pack of the pet dog is the family of people and other animals with which it lives. For a dog to be happy and acceptable to the rest of the pack, it needs a set of rules to live by. In the wild, these would be maintained by the stronger members of the pack. In the domestic situation, the humans take these roles.

For humans and dogs to live together successfully, the dog's owner must always be the pack leader, and the dog must be inferior to all human family members. Failure to impose this hierarchy can cause the dog to consider itself dominant to its owners. As a result, the dog will be difficult to train, behave in ways that are not socially acceptable in the family situation, and may even be dangerous. This will make the dog unpopular and a worry for the family, who will not understand its behavior and will consider it a "bad dog." It may mean that the dog has to be shut away much of the time, for example, for the safety of young children, and in the worst scenario, euthanized for bad behavior.

Why can't I be pack leader?

Dominance Training - For Owners

Not all dogs are the dominant type, but for those that are, prevention is easier than cure, and early establishment of a dog's place in the family pack will mean a happier relationship in the long term.

Walk through doorways in front of your dog. Do not step over or walk around the dog if it is in the way. Make the dog move.

Don't let the dog into your bedroom or onto your bed. Occasionally go and sit in the dog's bed. Do not allow the dog onto laps or furniture.

Never feed your dog from your plate or while you are eating. Feed the dog its own food after you have eaten.

? Why do I want to lick your face?

The opposite of the dominant dog is the submissive one. When puppies are young, they lick the muzzle of their mother to stimulate her to regurgitate food for them. While this is not necessary for puppies born in the domestic situation, the instinct remains. It is therefore normal behavior for a dog to want to lick the faces and hands of humans, as a sign of submission and affection. Because of possible health risks, this behavior should be discouraged, but gently so, bearing in mind that these are already submissive dogs. Distraction with a toy is a good alternative.

Always win any games. Give the dog attention when you initiate it, not when the dog asks for it.

Q. why do I get a treat when I do as I am told?

A

Attitudes toward dog training have changed dramatically in the last few years. It is now realized that, instead of punishing a dog for wrong behavior, dogs learn much more quickly (and less traumatically) if they are rewarded for getting it right. A dog's behavior is determined by the result the behavior brings, so if a certain behavior is followed by a good experience, that behavior will tend to be repeated. Conversely, if behavior is ignored and nothing gained from it, it will die out. Training based on a reward system for the correct responses enables dogs to learn in a positive way what humans want to teach them.

? *What rewards will you give me?*

Most dogs are very food-oriented, and small tasty treats make excellent rewards when training. These can be part of the dog's daily food ration or be healthy additions, such as pieces of carrot or morsels of baked liver. Lavish praise is also essential. All dogs want the approval of their pack leader — verbal praise and possibly physical contact are a great encouragement.

? *What will you do if I ignore you?*

This can be very frustrating when trying to train a dog, or to change some aspect of its behavior. However, the dog should not be punished.

It is possible that the dog did not understand the training command, which is therefore not its fault. To punish in this situation would cause more misunderstanding and be totally counterproductive.

Also, bear in mind that dogs have very short memory spans — around half a second — so by the time the dog is punished, it will not be aware of the reason for the punishment. It is better to use deterrents to emphasize the idea that behavior that is ignored or nonproductive should cease. Smacking dogs rarely achieves anything other than making the dog fearful or aggressive. To large dogs, it can even seem like boisterous play.

Good Dog!

Rewards reinforce good behavior; deterrents discourage poor behavior. Dogs should never be hit.

The timing of rewards is crucial, because a dog has such a short memory span. The reward should be given at the exact time of the correct response. Initially, rewards should be given every time the dog gets it right, then intermittently.

Deterrents are of two kinds. The first is to ignore the dog and its behavior totally. If that is insufficient, the dog can be socially isolated by being sent out of the room.

The second deterrent seeks to stop the dog's behavior by creating a surprise diversion, such as a sudden noise (perhaps by throwing training disks or a bunch of keys on the floor) or a squirt of water (aimed at the dog's body). The dog should be rewarded as soon as it stops the behavior.

Q. why must I learn to sit?

A A well-behaved dog is a pleasure to be with. Knowledge of a few basic commands makes a dog socially acceptable, and can keep it safe from danger. The important words are "Sit!" "Stay!" "Down!" and "Come!" Training can start at eight weeks of age, and should be carried out using rewards and praise. Begin with a daily training session of a few minutes. As the dog progresses, the sessions can occur once or twice a week. Once learned, response to a command should be instant.

Teaching a dog to sit can be easy using a tidbit as a lure. Hold the tidbit just out of reach above the dog's head. Sooner or later the dog will sit in order to look up and see the tidbit. All other behavior must be ignored. If necessary, hold the tidbit close to the dog's face, and then slowly raise it until the dog tilts its head up to look at the treat. The hindquarters will automatically go down. As the dog's bottom touches the ground, say "Sit!" When its bottom is properly on the ground, give it the tidbit. The command "Down!" can be taught in a similar way.

? And why do I have to learn to stay?

This command can save a dog's life. It may stop it from dashing across a street or under a tractor. The command should be said in a sharp tone, and the hand held out, palm downward. Command words should be consistent and not confusing for the dog. For example, "Down!" could mean either lie down or get down. To avoid misunderstanding, use another term for one of these.

? *I love digging in the yard. I wonder why this is?*

Digging is natural canine behavior, and is usually done to bury bones and other special "prizes" to prevent them from being taken by another animal. Some breeds of dog – terriers, for example – dig to catch rodents. The habit is usually unpopular with owners, and may be impossible to break, but it can be redirected by providing a special digging area, such as a sandpit in the yard.

No Jumping

Jumping up to greet humans is a friendly gesture. However, it is not an acceptable one, especially in larger breeds.

To train a dog out of jumping up, say "No!" sharply, followed by "Sit!" If the dog obeys, give it a treat. The dog may be encouraged to obey the "Sit!" command if it can see the treat in your hand. It is important that all visitors to the house adopt the same policy.

It may help if you greet your dog in a crouched position. Striking the dog with anything could seem like play, and actually encourage the jumping up.

Dogs that persist in jumping can be put on the leash to greet visitors, and need extra work on the commands "Sit!" and 'Down!" in their regular training sessions.

SPECIAL
FEATURE

Communication

Communication between humans uses more than just speech – body language and eye contact are equally important aspects of the way we express ourselves.

These forms of communication are even more vital for dogs, especially body language. Although dogs vocalize, they do not have a vocabulary. It is important that we learn to interpret what dogs are trying to communicate to us. It may prevent misunderstanding and inappropriate discipline; for example, a dog that appears stubborn may actually be apprehensive because of the frustration in our voice, when it has genuinely not understood what we wanted it to do.

Body Language

Dogs use many parts of their bodies when expressing themselves: ears, eyes, mouth, tail, whole body. The prime part is the tail. The angle at which it is held and how it is moved demonstrates whether a dog is happy, frightened, submissive, or about to attack. The ears also say a lot. In submission or pleasure, they are held back against the head. They are also in this position if a dog is about to attack, so it can be important to "read" the whole dog. An alert, listening dog will have pricked ears.

▲ **"Do I really have to sit here?" this young dog seems to be asking.**

Dogs use eye contact between themselves; a dominant dog may glare in disapproval at a lower-ranking dog, or give it a look of approval. Our dogs learn to read our eyes in the same way, and soon know whether we are looking at them in a cross, amused, or loving way. There is little doubt about a snarling dog. However, many dogs also expose their teeth when happy, and appear almost to be smiling. Body posture varies a great deal, depending on how the dog is feeling, from an aggressive stance when the dog tries to make itself appear larger, to a submissive crouch or roll.

A happy dog being stroked has its ears back and its eyes half closed. The whole body is relaxed, and the tail may wag. In a friendly greeting and during play, the dog seems to wag its entire body, its face appears happy, and it seeks eye contact. A frightened dog has its tail between its legs and the back end lowered. It avoids eye contact by keeping the eyes down, with an apprehensive look in them. A frightened dog may tremble and shake, and if very nervous, may relieve itself. A submissive dog tends to slink or crawl along with its belly on the ground and then roll over, exposing its tummy when approached. The ears are flattened, and the tail may be wagged in a friendly gesture.

An aggressive dog stands soundly, often with the hairs around the neck and along the back – the "hackles" – raised. It stares, its lips may be drawn back, and it may be growling. The tail is held stiffly out.

Vocalization

Vocalization as a means of communication is used much more by some dogs than others. We all know the growl of aggression. However, some dogs make low growling noises when happy, and many "talk" to their owners for several minutes, though what they are saying is anyone's guess. It is probable that they do this because it elicits a pleasurable response from the owners.

▲ The ear positions and facial changes of this dog range expressively from mild disinterest, through pleasurable expectation, to disappointment.

▲ The body language of the Jack Russell is clearly one of vociferous, happy confidence, unlike the uncertainty the two young dogs are displaying.

Why don't you chase me when I run

A

This sort of behavior is 100 percent attention seeking. Choosing an item it shouldn't have, such as its owner's shoe, virtually guarantees getting attention and being pursued, which is exactly what the dog wants. If the behavior is totally ignored, it will be unproductive and stop.

off with your shoe

Start the recall training when the dog is hungry, so that the reward of food is a good incentive to come back to you. Besides giving it a treat, praise the dog and greet it affectionately. Treats can be given randomly, sometimes after two recalls, sometimes after five.

Having established recall at home, try it in a more open environment. There will be many more distractions here, so put the dog on a long extending leash at first. Once you are satisfied with its response, you can let it off the leash.

Come Here!

Recall should always be associated with a pleasant experience, such as a treat, play with a favorite toy, or a fuss from a happy, smiling owner.

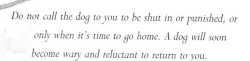

Do not call the dog to you to be shut in or punished, or only when it's time to go home. A dog will soon become wary and reluctant to return to you.

? *Why do I chew things?*

Most puppies go through a chewing stage that starts when they are changing their teeth. For some dogs, this chewing habit persists into adulthood. There are various ways to stop the habit. Puppies can be encouraged to chew items that its owner selects, and discouraged from chewing others. Chew toys should not be anything that can be confused with household items. A strong-tasting deterrent spray put onto unacceptable items may help. As a last resort, a chewing dog can be distracted by a loud noise, or a squirt of water from a water pistol or squirt bottle aimed at its body. Chewing dogs can be left in house cages with chews when the owners go out.

? *I like chasing rabbits. Why should I come back to you instead?*

The chase instinct is very strong in some dogs. However, it can get them into serious trouble, cause a public nuisance, and leave the owner fuming with frustration. To prevent or overcome this behavior, the dog must be trained to obey the recall signal. This is an important part of early training, and can be started at home as soon as the dog responds to its name. The dog's name should be used exclusively to recall it at first, so that it associates its name with coming back to its owner and not with any other stimulus. Alternatively, another signal, such as a whistle, can be used. A dog will not want to return to a reprimand, so however long it takes the dog to come back, it should always be rewarded for that return.

i have more fun off the

A

With very few exceptions, dogs need to be on a leash at some point in their lives. For many dogs, especially those that live in residential areas, the leash is a legal requirement. Early familiarization with a leash is therefore of great benefit, and can be started in puppyhood. There are many sorts of leash. The most familiar attach to the dog's collar, and are also available in extendible versions that give the dog greater freedom. There are choke collars, which hurt the dog when tugged quickly by the handler and hopefully discourage it from pulling away. Head halters give more control over the dog's head, so that when it pulls forward, the head is pulled down. Lastly, there are harnesses, some of which have an anti-pulling effect. Choke collars could injure the spine if used too vigorously, and there are kinder and more effective methods of leash training.

I have more fun off the leash.
Must I have one

? 99

leash. Must I have one?

Heel!

A dog that walks to heel is a pleasure to take out.

Teaching a dog to walk to heel can be started in the yard without a leash. Walk around, holding a treat in your hand so that your dog knows it is there. This will cause the dog to walk beside you, and as it does, say "Heel!" several times and give it treats.

? *You* walk so slowly, it's not surprising that I pull on the leash. Why shouldn't I?

There are two main reasons why dogs pull away. One is to reach a goal quickly, such as its favorite location or another dog. The other is that the dog considers itself to be in charge of the walk, and in a position to dictate the pace and direction of it. If the incentive can be decreased, the pulling can also be decreased, so it is useful to examine why the dog is pulling away.

To keep a dog from pulling on the leash, one of the special anti-pulling harnesses and a system of rewards can be effective. Another option is to walk backward. Using a regular or extendible leash connected to the collar, begin the walk. As the dog starts to pull, begin to walk backward. This will tighten the leash and surprise the dog, who will come trotting back. When it does, reward and praise the dog. This will take several sessions, but can be very successful.

Once this is established, keep the treats out of sight, but still reward the dog for walking to heel. Next, practice the exercise with the dog on a leash. Walking to heel is a boring exercise for the dog, so keep the training sessions short — approximately five minutes.

A ?. I feel really upset when left alone. Why?

Some dogs become agitated when left alone. They are suffering from a condition known as separation anxiety. It can happen in dogs that have become overdependent on one or more of their owners. It also occurs when dogs are suddenly faced with periods alone, having previously always had company; for example, both adults in the family going out to work once all the children have started school. Occasionally, fear of being alone is felt by dogs that have undergone a bad experience, such as a burglary.

? Why do I behave so badly?

Dogs suffering from separation anxiety display a variety of behaviors. Some bark and howl in an attempt to call back other members of their pack. Some become destructive, chewing the furniture, digging at carpets, and scratching doors. The digging and chewing are displacement activities resulting from anxiety. The scratching at doors may be an attempt to escape and follow the owner. The destruction often happens just after the owner has gone out. Some dogs soil the house in their distress.

I feel really upset
when left alone. Why   ?
101

Start to leave the dog alone for short periods from an early age. Accustom the dog to being shut in another room while people are at home.

Prevent overdependence by not allowing your dog access to you 24 hours a day. Accustom your dog to going into a crate or pen from an early age. This can give the dog a feeling of security, and prevents destructive behavior.

? *Is there any treatment that can help me?*

Dogs with separation anxiety can be helped. The first step is to identify the cause, if possible. In the majority of cases, it is overdependence on the owner, so reducing this will help the dog to cope with being left alone. Weaning the dog away from its dependence needs to done very gradually, and starts with the dog being separated from the owner while both are at home. To help the dog feel more secure, a crate often helps. The dog can become accustomed to the crate while the owner is at home, and then for short spells alone. Chews will be a distraction, and an item with the owner's smell on it may be a comfort. A radio or television can be left on. There is medication available from the veterinarian to help these dogs, but it needs to be used in conjunction with behavioral therapy to be effective.

Home Alone

Separation anxiety is distressing for both dog and owner. It can be prevented.

Don't make a fuss when going out and returning — this can exacerbate both the excitement and the anxiety the dog feels. And, most important, don't punish a dog for misdeeds done when alone — this will only increase its anxiety.

Symptoms and Ailments

Most well-cared-for pet dogs live a long and healthy life. If something does go wrong, however, prompt action by the owner could mean the difference between life and death. In some situations, such as an accident or viral infection, a dog's condition can deteriorate very quickly. In other situations, an owner's careful observations of the dog can provide the veterinarian with much essential information, which will help him or her to make a swift diagnosis.

This section gives a list of symptoms, together with possible ailments and suggestions of what owners should do. There is also a code indicating how serious the symptoms are. Remember, though, if the dog is in pain or distress, or if you are unsure what is wrong, take the dog to the veterinarian immediately.

KEY

 Keep dog under observation for 3–4 days. If symptoms persist, make an appointment with the veterinarian.

 Keep dog under observation for 24–48 hours. If symptoms do not improve, contact veterinarian.

 Take dog to veterinarian if there is no improvement within 12 hours, or if condition worsens.

 Take dog to veterinarian immediately. This is an emergency.

SYMPTOM	POSSIBLE CAUSES	OWNER ACTION	KEY
ABDOMINAL DISTENSION *Acute*	Gastric dilation, trauma, hemorrhage	Act promptly	● ● ● ●
Slowly increasing	Pregnancy, constipation, enlarged organs, tumor, fluid in abdomen	Look for other signs, eg, nipple enlargement, cough	●
ALOPECIA	Demodex mites, hormone imbalance, excessive licking and scratching by dog	Observe dog and check for fleas	●
APPETITE *Increase in, with weight gain*	Overfeeding, steroid therapy, metabolic disorder	Weigh daily food ration carefully. Weigh dog weekly	●
Increase in, with weight loss	Diabetes, malabsorption, increased metabolic demands, eg, pregnancy	Observe feces and water intake	●
Loss of	Fever, infection, pain, anxiety, hot weather, gastrointestinal disorder, organ failure, eg, kidney	Observe for other signs	● ●
BAD BREATH	Eating feces, dental disease, oral infection	Stop the habit. Look in mouth and at teeth	●
BLEEDING *From mouth*	Trauma, infection	Look in mouth	● ●
From nose	Trauma, clotting disorder, persistent infection, tumor	Keep nose down. Place ice pack on muzzle	● ● ● ●

In feces	Colitis, neoplasia	Collect sample	● ●
In urine	Cystitis, stones, trauma, tumor	Collect sample	● ● ●
BOTTOM DRAGGING ALONG GROUND	Anal sacs full or infected	Check area for soreness and fleas	● ●
BREATHING *Noisy*	Partial airway obstruction	Check if it is worse at rest or during exercise	● ●
Rapid	Hemorrhage, fear, respiratory disease, cardiac disease, metabolic disorder, brain disease	Stay calm. Look at color of mucous membrane	● ● ● ●
CHEWING ITSELF	Allergic skin disease, anal sacs full, fleas	Look for fleas	●
CONSTIPATION	Pain, poor food intake, bowel obstruction, muscle weakness	Look for straining	● ● ● ●
CONVULSIONS	Epilepsy, poisoning, metabolic problem, head trauma, tumor	Note duration of convulsion and any loss of consciousness	● ● ● ●
COUGH	Bronchitis, heart disease, infection, eg, kennel cough, parasites, eg, lungworm	Keep away from other dogs until cause known	● ●
DIARRHEA	Bacterial/viral infection, parasites, food intolerance, maldigestion/malabsorption, tumors, poison	Note how often dog defecates per day, nature of feces, and if there is any blood	● ●

	Possible cause	What to do	
DISCHARGE *Ear*	Infection of outer ear canal	Clean carefully with a cotton ball	● ●
Eye	Conjunctivitis	Wipe with plain, boiled water	● ●
Nose	Foreign body, tumor, infection – bacterial, viral, or fungal	Note whether from one or both nostrils	●
Penis	Infection of prepuce or urinary tract; discharge is normal in some dogs	Look for swelling	●
Vulva	Heat cycle, vaginitis, pyometra	If bitch has not been spayed and is not in heat, act promptly	● ● ● ●
DRINKING EXCESSIVELY	Fever, kidney disease, diabetes, pyometra, adrenal gland disorder	Measure water intake over 24 hours and collect urine sample	● ●
EAR *Held down*	Infection, foreign body	Check ear for smell and discharge	● ●
Odor	Dirty ear, infection	Look in ear and note any redness or discharge	● ●
Scratching	Ear infection, foreign body, allergic skin disease	Check ear for discharge	● ●
EYE *Opaque*	Corneal problem, cataract	Observe whether eye appears painful	● ● ● ●

Red	Inflammation of conjunctiva, blood in eye	Look closely to see which part is red	● ●	
Semi-closed	Painful eye, foreign body, trauma	Bathe with plain, boiled water	● ● ●	
Third eyelid up	Ocular problem or sign of general ill health	Look for other signs	● ● ● ●	
Wet and runny	Irritation to eye	Check eye for obvious foreign bodies	● ● ●	
FACIAL SWELLING	Allergic reaction to insect sting, abscess	Observe how quickly it develops	● ● ● ●	
FLATULENCE	Diet that does not suit dog, eating trash, old age	Change food and feed 2–4 times a day	●	
GUMS **Bleed easily**	Dental disease, infection, clotting disorder	Check teeth	● ● ●	
Sore	Gingivitis	Feed soft food	●	
HEAD **Shaking**	Foreign body, nasal irritation	Look for other signs	● ● ● ●	
Tilting	Disturbance of balance, ear or brain problem	Note if dog is wobbly or circling	● ● ●	

INCONTINENCE	Damage to nerves to bladder, urethral sphincter problem, prostate gland enlargement, excessive drinking	Observe if worse when dog is standing or lying down, and obtain urine sample	●
JAUNDICE	Liver disease, tumor, anemia	Check color of conjunctiva in eye	● ● ●
LAMENESS *Front leg*	Developmental problems, eg, short radius	Assess severity of lameness and pain felt	● ●
Hind leg	Hip dysplasia, patellar luxation	Strict rest	● ●
Painful and acute lameness in any leg	Sprain, fracture, dislocation, arthritis, bone tumor, developmental problems	Strict rest	● ● ● ●
LETHARGY	Many reasons for this, eg, heart disease, anemia	Look for other symptoms	●
LOSS OF CONSCIOUSNESS	Head injury, epilepsy, faint, diabetic coma, intracranial hemorrhage	Keep dog warm and check airway is clear	● ● ● ●
LUMPS	Fatty lumps, warts, abscess, hernia, skin tumor	Feel for heat and pain	● ●
MAMMARY GLANDS, LUMPS	Benign lumps, malignant tumors	Examine all ten glands for lumps	● ●
MOUTH *Dribbling*	Loose tooth, foreign body in mouth, infection, trauma	Open mouth and look in, if possible	● ● ● ●

Pawing at	Something stuck in mouth	Open mouth and look in, if possible	● ● ●
NOSE, WARM AND DRY	Fever, old age	Assess general health	●
PANTING	Fever, excitement, heatstroke, fear, hormonal disorder	Make sure dog is able to cool off, and give reassurance	● ● ●
REGURGITATION	Eating too fast, esophageal obstruction, megaesophagus	Try feeding 2–3 small meals per day	●
RELUCTANCE TO EXERCISE	Pain, cardiac disease, metabolic disease	Look for stiffness or other signs	●
SALIVATION, DRIBBLING	Rabies, foreign body	Check roof of mouth for possible wedged object	● ● ● ●
SCRATCHING	Fleas, mites, allergic skin disease	Look for fleas/flea dirt	●
SKIN *Scabby/spotty*	Self-inflicted by scratching, infection, mites, autoimmune skin disease	Observe dog to see if itchy	●
Scaly	Parasites, seborrhea, dietary imbalance, excessive bathing	Discuss problem with veterinarian	●
Swelling	Abscess, lump	Feel for heat	● ●

Symptom	Possible causes	Action		
SNEEZING	Upper respiratory tract infection, nasal irritation	Look for nasal discharge	●	●
SQUATTING FREQUENTLY	Cystitis, diabetes, pyometra, kidney disease	Obtain urine sample	●	●
STRAINING TO DEFECATE	Constipation, prostate gland enlargement, colitis, bowel obstruction	Observe bowel habits	● ●	● ●
SWALLOWING, DIFFICULTY IN	Trauma, tumors, pain, eg, sore mouth	Check mouth and offer soft food	●	●
TEMPERATURE, RAISED	Infection, leukemia, autoimmune disease, poison	Offer plenty of fresh water	● ●	●
URINATION, EXCESSIVE	Urinary tract infection, diabetes, kidney disease	Make plenty of water available	●	●
VOMITING	Gastrointestinal inflammation, obstruction, motion sickness, poisoning, dietary indiscretion	Remember what your dog ate	● ●	●
WEAKNESS	Cardiac disease, metabolic problem, neurological disease, hormone disorder, old age	Note any other symptoms	●	
WEIGHT *Gain*	Overfeeding, inactivity, pregnancy, hormonal imbalance	Weigh weekly and measure food intake	●	
Loss	Inadequate amount of food, difficulty eating, vomiting, impaired digestion and absorption	Feed 2–3 meals of high-energy food per day	●	

Index